FOOTBALL DELIRIUM

T0347866

FOOTBALL DELIRIUM

Chris Oakley

Routledge
Taylor & Francis Group

LONDON AND NEW YORK

First published 2007 by
Karnac Books Ltd.

Published 2018 by Routledge
2 Park Square, Milton Park, Abingdon, Oxon OX14 4RN
711 Third Avenue, New York, NY 10017, USA

Routledge is an imprint of the Taylor & Francis Group, an informa business

British Library Cataloguing in Publication Data
A C.I.P. for this book is available from the British Library

ISBN-13 9781780491820 (pbk)

Edited, designed, and produced by Florence Production Ltd
www.florenceproduction.co.uk

CONTENTS

Introduction

I am sitting in a rather dusty cricket stadium in Dacca in
Bangladesh. It is November 2003, but it could have been
yesterday. I am idly watching "Freddy" Flintoff batter the
young Bangladeshi bowlers to all parts of the ground. A couple
of seats up from me sits a young man. Presumably a local.
Equally idly glancing at a newspaper, occasionally looking up
to gaze, faintly forlornly, at the cricket. The newspaper is,
appropriately enough, entirely written in Bengali, which is
completely and irretrievably incomprehensible to me. But then,
suddenly, seemingly apropos of nothing, he leans over and
nudges me in the ribs. Speaking no English, he points animatedly
at a somewhat smudgy photo, and breaks out into a huge grin.
There, peering out from the Bengali hieroglyphics, are the
unmistakable features of that global icon, at that time the most
marketable man of the moment. By now, as is the way of such
things, he has become a little "last year". The man, who a
friend of mine, engaging in a compulsive imitation of the English
High Court judge, insists on calling "Beckenham". And there we
are, just for that moment, exchanging grins and nodding. The
language of communication, the medium that this exchange

1

takes place within, is that which is now everywhere. Ubiquitous is the word. Football. Or as some affectionately refer to it: "Footy". Offering, amidst other possibilities, a sanctuary, a sense of place, a community, a language. And for so many of us, an addiction, a self-elected madness. But we are getting ahead of ourselves.

A few months earlier an extraordinarily wealthy Russian was sitting in one of London's most expensive restaurants. He was a comparatively young man, and the impatience that can so often accompany youth was getting the better of him. Hesitations and indecisions were becoming increasingly trying for our man as representatives of Tottenham Hotspur Football Club appeared to dither over the details, the guarantees or lack of them, of the offer that was on the table. The exquisite truffle omelette followed by the tender liver had done little to improve his mood. He was in town to broker a deal. He was a business man, an enormously successful one. Six months later a chocolate shop in Moscow would create half a dozen miniature chocolate figurines depicting the most wealthy and influential men in Russia. And he would be among them. Clearly he was no fool but he was not, by any stretch of the imagination, a "football man". But as a man who led the markets he knew a market leader when he saw one. And he wanted in on it, be part of the buzz, the mood of the moment. He knew that there was a worldwide obsession with football. What is more is that he knew that via an association with it there was potential for a certain celebrity and the opening of doors for a whole host of burgeoning business possibilities. And following him, a whole host of others brandishing obscene sums of money are now only too eager to get in on the act. What he did not know, and in all probability did not concern himself with overmuch, was "why?" Why this worldwide preoccupation? Does anybody have the answer? It would appear that football has claws, for the world as we know it, is possessed. Somehow it never lets go, and not merely the sports pages are in danger of being swallowed by its hungry sprawl. For many what is in play is seizure, rapture, demonic possession, frenzy, delirium, in more or less manageable doses. Although of course, just as the effects of the psychoanalytic tie are hardly containable to the classical fifty minute "hour", nor are these football passions bounded by the standard ninety minutes of any particular game.

Today I receive a postcard from a friend, who it so happens is another psychoanalyst but who, as yet, knows nothing of this book. He and his wife have been up in Northern Thailand and he writes, jovially, of being "beyond the Beckham factor". Such places are rapidly shrinking, for the escapist activity has become nigh on inescapable. But if psychoanalysis, or at least this psychoanalyst, is going to have something to say about this football phenomenon, two things seem potentially unforgivable: firstly, to "shrink", to reduce football and an excessive interest in it under the heading of psychopathology. After all, I'm a fully paid up member of that club, the club of the obsessives, although that in itself, would hardly rule out the pathological. Nevertheless so often this fascination may be the liveliest thing about a particular individual, the place where they seem to become most exuberant. In other words, to be on the side of health.

Secondly the other crime would be to use football, rather like a poor case history, to buttress some rather shaky theoretical speculations. Sometimes it seems as if psychoanalysis, by its emphasis on the unspeakable, the unspoken aspects of our being, loosely speaking what we are "unconscious of", is proposing a life beyond ordinary restraint. To facilitate a negotiation between the shameful and the shameless. So if football has become a medium through which certain aspects of our being, certain anxieties and certain appetites or desires, can find expression, maybe that's just fine. In other words it is not through an analysis of football that there is any therapeutic intent, no desire to change anything at all. Or put another way there may be ways in which we are together that are concealed, that are embedded in football, and that it is important to acknowledge an entitlement to that.

As Thomas Nagel writes "each of our inner (or private) lives is such a jungle of thoughts, feelings, fantasies, and impulses that civilisation would be impossible if we expressed them all or if we could read each other's minds." So if football is the form in which some of us find a hard-earned way of expressing some of these "thoughts, feelings and fantasies and impulses", a way of reminding ourselves of a whole host of unforgettable satisfactions, so be it.

Football has become manifestly more visible and more central to certainly an English way of life, but simultaneously this is true for almost everywhere else. The one location that sustains a resistance, a good old fashioned psychoanalytical term, is the United States. They are one of the few countries that refer to the game as "soccer", possible reasons for this antipathy we shall examine later. But elsewhere the major teams and the star players are rarely out of the news, more often than not for the "wrong" reasons, sustaining football as one of the insistent soap operas of our time. So the sort of questions that psychoanalysis might very well ask of football is what is it being used for? What might be said about the function that it provides for so many of us? What sort of "place" is it? What might a sustained interrogation reveal? Interrogation always being entangled in a concern with justice.

A tentative or preliminary answer heads off in the following direction: it seems to me that, whatever else football may be involved in, it operates insistently as dream space . . . a place apart, something other. This we seek to sustain as bright, as luminous even, whilst simultaneously we can find ourselves cornered in some other reality: football becoming the taste of colour in a wash of grey. Football, as the writer and film maker Iain Sinclair says of walking, "frees the spirit and delights the eye." Any which way, lace up the boots. It allows us, as communion, as community, to share a whole catalogue of intensely intoxicating sense impressions in-mixed with heightened emotions. Those adrenaline moments. It is, after all—just as psychoanalysis should be—great fun, and yet at times it will bring about immense depression, anguish and despair. Catastrophic dismay and barely containable grief haunt the terrain.

But of greater significance is that football offers us the possibility of manageable doses of self-elected madness. A madness that is essential for a sane life. For the paradox is that this very madness is simultaneously therapeutic: football as an insistent provocation, repeatedly re-inaugurating reverie or drift, disrupted by those moments of the most intense fracture, moments of the autistic stare. Proffering a roller-coaster of intense discomfort, anguish ecstasies interspersed with abstracted longings so redolent of the back ward in-patient, forever lurking in the discontinued corridors of our old lunatic asylums. Yet always present, just round the corner, lies the possibility of almost uncontainable happiness, always an abundance, always an overflowing. Simultaneously football provides us with our own utterly personal and yet simultaneously collective—as in programmed—delusional system: a universe organised around the fixtures. For vast swathes of the population football sets up an unrelenting conflict, a form of queasiness in the face of this madness which so possesses, so enraptures, so appropriates, so grips. Indulgent fantasies of escape proliferate. Of reeling away from a sub-culture that seems to be making not merely a virtue but a set of principles out of banality overlaying the beautiful. Attempts at extrication, for the most part, founder, collapsing into muttered polemic that continues to be half entranced by what is so denounced.

Whilst never forgetting those delirious moments of abundant happiness that football has the potential to provide, it is crucial to recognise the other end of the continuum: grief. The power of grief to derange the mind has been extensively noted. And it is an essential ingredient in what football proposes. Freud in his 1917 *Mourning and Melancholia* suggested that the act of grieving "involves grave departures from the normal attitude to life."

Nevertheless he pointed out that grief is sustained as differing from other derangement, "It never occurs to us to regard it as a pathological condition and refer it to medical treatment." There is an unwavering reliance on "its being overcome after a certain lapse of time . . . any interference with it (is seen) as useless and even harmful." And all this over the loss of what? A particular game? It's as shallow, as trivial as that. But for the most part this has faded, like the newspaper reports with their ability to provoke a further wave, another paroxysm, all destined for the recycling bin; all superimposed by the advent of . . . the next game. Melanie Klein writing in 1940 in *Mourning and its Relation to Manic-Depressive States* came to a similar conclusion: "The mourner is in fact ill, but because this state of mind is common and seems natural to us, we do not call mourning an illness . . . to put my conclusion more precisely: I should say that in mourning the subject goes through a modified and transitory manic-depressive state and overcomes it." And crazy though it may seem, or pathetic in the eyes of those unaffected by such contagions, this is one aspect of the madness that football consigns us to, and that we, willingly for the most part, sign up for.

In the chapters that follow we will trace out further elements that inform the "football phenomenon", some of which almost need no introduction. So often it is said that in times of comparative "peace" it offers an outlet for our warring impulses. This will be examined in the chapter "Trenchmouth". Similarly it is hardly an original claim (see "Losing: My Religion") that in a secular age football operates as a substitute religion, often by proposing a possibility of what we all "believe in": the possibility of belonging, the possibility of community. Again nothing prevents the thought that a whole set of sexual concerns, whether in terms of masculine identity or the possibilities for sublimation that football provides, can be played out ("Sex in the Stadium"). And that ultimately the heady mix of aesthetic and the athletic combine to provide what is essential for our well being: a play space ("Parklife"). But above all, right at the centre of the phenomenon, is this issue of containable doses of madness that are in themselves enormously therapeutic: football is the therapy that so many of us are in.

Madness seemingly holds an enormous appeal for painters, poets and novelists. Perhaps this is true for so many of us, particularly those who have managed to sustain a comforting distance from the excruciating and demoralising ordeal of having a hands-on involvement with the mentally derailed. As Susan Sontag so shrewdly remarked "depression is melancholy without the charm". A view emphatically held by the Aston Villa management during Stan *("Tackling the Demons")* Collymore's psychological collapse. But the mythologies of madness prevail, all sustained by a considerable literature. There is a curious sense that the insanity that suffused the lives of so many philosophers, composers, and literary figures (so often in the nineteenth century, brought on by tertiary syphilis, and its link to sexual excess) both illuminates their work and simultaneously suggests something of a superior sensibility. As if by going mad Nietzsche or Schumann had opted to scorch their souls in the pursuit of a beautiful truth. Cue Cantona and the rush of blood, the kung-fu lunge on that dark night at Selhurst Park.

Incontestably there has been a romanticization of madness. The realm of the psychopathic is consistently elevated to the position of the ultimate alternative life-style: "million-airhead" footballers play their part, tawdry relics of a hooligan past regurgitate paperback narratives of violence addictions, and the film maker Van Sant drools over the last lost days of Kurt Cobain, with Hunter Davies following suit with Paul Gascoigne. And somewhere lodged in this (although allow a potential fading), is that figure of mystique and dubious status, the strutting lay priesthood in a secular age: the psychiatrist and the psychoanalyst. Inevitably the charge of facetiousness in this linking of football and madness lurks just over the horizon. As if such a thesis only too easily moves into the slipstream of the prevailing fascination with the deviant and the dysfunctional. To utilise the term madness too glibly will always run the risk of sustaining the long-standing tradition of situating the disturbed and the disturbing on the periphery of our concerns. Perhaps the more apposite term is that football is *mental.* Phrases such as "And the crowd go wild" as their team "run riot" suggest a riotous wildness that operates as an unceasing potentiality.

Nothing prevents the thought that football always allows a sustained involvement with our childhood. It is, after all, only a game. But those aspects of our childhood under scrutiny are more infantile than any sport. For it is in infancy that some psychoanalysts wish to claim that once upon a time we were all a little mad. But more importantly we never really grow out of it. Certain phases or positions are designated, in particular the so-called "paranoid-schizoid position" which if all goes well will eventually transmute into the forlornly named "depressive position". The latter proposing a stage where we will have developed a capacity for concern for others. But prior to that there will be a veritable tempest of torment and destructive ecstasies that will hold sway: precisely the lot of both player and spectator during the typical ninety minutes and beyond. Without getting too technical the "paranoid-schizoid" phase has certain immutable characteristics: an unawareness of others (the gimlet eyed glare accompanied by the venomous bark of "break his fucking leg"); "splitting" (lopping off unpleasant aspects of oneself and lodging them with the other, along the lines of "All Chelsea are NF bastards", "Wenger is a fucking paedophile", and "Have you ever seen (Sol) Campbell with a bird?"); and last but not least a prevalence of paranoid anxiety (at times quite palpable in the away end at Old Trafford—how many seasons did it take before an away side was awarded a penalty up in Manchester?).

The psychoanalyst most associated with this line of thinking is Melanie Klein and she was most explicit that the term "position" is used advisedly because none of this is a passing phase or stage. For her there will always be underlying paranoid and depressive anxieties for us all. No escape from these encrypted enclaves of madness. And even a cursory glance at most football followers would seem to bear this out.

There appears to be a general consensus that a repressed life is an unhappy life. But equally one without restraint, despite our envy of the psychopath, or some form of self containment, will rendezvous with crushing disappointment. So if it holds true that this crucial element of our human condition—an originary core of madness—is inescapable, is there not a very real imperative that it calls for some manageable forms of expression? A "better out than in" principle? Madness comes in many forms, and not all are to be designated as sick. Football facilitates a set of co-existing possibilities, for it is here that we can be mad to be out of it, out of the exhilarating yet conflicting perplexities of sexual politics. We can be "mad for it", a compulsive desire to once again hitch ourselves to that voluntary or involuntary immersion, the desire to go on tilt. Mad, less on the side of something regressive, but now a progress narrative, suggesting an unstaunchable eagerness and urgency to cast off the constraining carapace of identity: to be everyone, to be swept up via the contagions of the game into a borderless sea of identifications that obliterate identity. Mad to be entranced, and entranced by the madness. Perhaps madness is too generic, perhaps the more specific term should be delirium. Therapeutic delirium.

So what can be said about this distinctive culture of controlled dementia? What of its contradictions, its coherences? How does it work, resist change and yet constantly change? What can we make of the national game, the global game, this game of games, the only game in town? Indeed, to touch on certain convergences between psychoanalysis and football, I am reminded that when in psychoanalytic supervision it was this latter phrase, "the only game in town", that was affectionately used not about football (my supervisor's other game was sailing) but about psycho-analysis itself. But I am straying, for what is proposed in this book is that football is the site, the subject, the occasion of what psychoanalysis purports to be: a thinking.

Psychoanalysis is still feared and attacked. And long may this be the case, because of course this is both a sign of and a stimulus to the sustained vitality of the project. In other words psycho-analysis is a bit threatening, or at least psychoanalysts like to think so. In part because it raises the "scandal" of our children's sex lives. But also the "scandal" that we all have sex lives. Which is not to say that we all are having sex. Clearly for some it is football where we are "having it off". In part the threat is because of the oedipal suggestion that we all want to have sex with our mothers and fathers; but also because it insists on making our world one in which there are potentialities of there being just too many variables to cope with. For some this is particularly anxiety arousing. For others it is of irresistible interest. And at times it can seem if football sets in play just too many variables. At the very least superficially the two principle forms of involvement in it, either playing or watching, appear to head off in somewhat divergent directions.

Supporting or playing for a team constitutes evidence that the person belongs to a specific group. It automatically installs the notion of a group life. At times for those followers of the largest and most successful clubs, an almost limitlessly large group. To lay claim to that is at one level to lay claim to an identity, to inclusion. It's tribal. But similarly it really does not matter whether the club is large or small, for it is precisely that: it is joining a "club". A club of those who seek to escape from those conformist concerns with oneself. As football tends towards being a "team game" (even in the kick-about variety of "three and in" there is a tendency to split up into sides), it lends itself to this issue of belonging. And this holds true whenever one plays. Invariably one plays for a particular team and a whole set of attachments, however momentarily, are set in play. And simultaneously a whole set of opposing positions. A very common phenomenon in clubs that run a number of teams is that a conflict emerges when a player is promoted to a higher XI. This is often met with that crucial psychoanalytic term, resistance, principally turning around this concern with belonging. Resistance to being returned, however momentarily, to the place of the outsider. Suffused with all the attendant anxieties of self-consciousness and concern with acceptance.

Similarly psychoanalysis itself, as a community or set of differing communities, offers similar possibilities for club joining. For example you have the "Freudians", or Melanie's lot, the "Kleinians", or those who like to drape a more continental scarf around their necks: followers of the "Lacanian" orientation.

Just as an individual contrives a style, a collection of images the purpose of which is integration, the effect of which is presentation, representation, so the football community—however fragmented—projects an appearance, a particular style. It sets forth a continuum of possibility that ranges from the Gary Lineker clean cut, "crisp" image with the faint trace of the halo effect, to the cocaine-snorting, misogynistic "Essex" man so skilfully ironised in the TV series *Footballers' Wives*. Always in conflict, it is made of various layers. At the bottom, the fundament, are the unchanging assumptions that as a sport it must adhere to certain eternal values, fictionalised around notions of "fair play" or "playing the game". Up nearer the surface floats fashion, whether in haircuts, length of shorts or a particular stylistic flourish such as bending the ball with the outside of the boot or shirt-tugging. Then always frothing on top are the fads: inflatable black puddings on the terraces of Bury for example, which make an appearance only to fade into a seriality of nostalgic smirks.

All is devoted to serving the particular interests of the prevailing culture. All of which is saturated subliminally with how the human condition is to be usefully engaged with, to be played with . . . "if man were never to fade away . . . but lingered on for ever in the world, how things would lose their power to move us. The most precious thing in life is its uncertainty." Yoshida Kenko's words in his *Essays in Idleness*, written in the 1330s, have been ceaselessly echoed, and whatever else football brings to the table it is this insistent uncertainty. Again, one of the immutables. After all who could have predicted the Zidane head-butt. It is utterly foundational, without it the delirium principle just cannot operate. And yet operating as a curious counterpoint is that, by and large (rather like having one's own name), once someone has nominated the team that they support, this remains unwavering, utterly certain. Like a marriage that would brook no thought of possible divorce or separation. A sort of "till death us do part". Once an "Evertonian", always an "Evertonian", that sort of thing. Again, curiously it is quite rare for psychoanalysts to change their allegiances. By and large people are in for the duration. As if there is some call for an anchoring point that enables the possibility of losing oneself in the madness. You don't have to be around football for very long for this obligatory delirium to reveal itself, to become manifestly transparent.

Yet there are occasions, umpteen occasions when there has to be an exercise in considerable patience to discern quite where it resides. One autumnal Friday evening I am in Limerick taking in a run of the mill Irish second division game. Limerick were faintly hovering on the edge of a promotion race but only the seriously deluded would claim that there was much at stake. The game was routine, routinely dreadful, a lot of huffing and puffing and much hopeful punting the ball in the general direction of the opposition's goal. Occasionally there would be little outbursts of almost polite clapping in acknowledgment of something that disrupted the tedium: the odd flash of skill or a particularly sustained bit of endeavour. I was reminded of how formal the Irish can be, of their love of show bands, of the black tie hotel "do" on a Saturday night. But one would have been hard put to discern any evidence of madness, of delirium, of excess in any shape or form. As the soft rain drifted in from the Atlantic it all felt almost tranquil, tranquilised. But to remove one's gaze from the game itself, to its wider environs, to the specificity of its localised context, you could begin to get a whiff of something else. Limerick and poverty have been graphically portrayed by Frank McCourt in his novel *Angela's Ashes* but contemporary Limerick, despite it's historical legacy of fascism and anti-Semitism running back to before the First World War and its reputation as a drug-fuelled, gang-based roughhouse, has a justifiable civic pride. But something had run out by the time you got to the football ground. Peter Miles has this to say in his handbook for Irish football stadia ". . . the ground would not look out of place on a TV news report from a war zone. Rubble and lumps of concrete lie everywhere and the dressing room appears to have been the victim of a direct hit . . . the League of Ireland does not do itself any favours by allowing grounds in this state to be used." That's as maybe, but the description is howitzer accurate, and the evening at Hogan Park was beginning, if one took ones eye off the ball as it were, to take shape as only too ample testimony to the resilience of the wounded mind.

But if supporting a team, as has been pointed out, is a recipe for disappointment, an invitation to inevitable grieving, what is this support supporting? Does it not look unequivocally perverse? What of the tears of the Newcastle United followers as their Championship dreams turned to ashes a few seasons back? Were they a way of softening the heart for the possibility of another wound? Hardly tears of joy for the possibility of fresh love, a fresh repertoire of images, once the next season began. Or were they a source of auto-erotic pleasure, or just unadulterated, unbridled grief? Let us not forget that so much of psychoanalytic theorising turns around these issues of loss. The axiom that "weaning always comes too soon" suffuses the literature. I was once told by a young woman, on her initial appointment, that on being referred to me she had been told that carved over the door to my consulting room was the phrase "Disappointment guaranteed". (Possibly an effect of the credit sequences that I was in the habit of running past in the talks, the teaching that I was involved with at the time, paying tribute to precisely that phrase stencilled onto a banner draped at the back of the stage at Genesis P. Orridge's Throbbing Gristle gigs.)

Curious one might think that she came along nevertheless, and continued to come. But not so curious if we underline what Adam Phillips draws attention to in his introduction to Freud's *Wild Analysis*, "Freud was not a pessimist, but he was a great writer about the nature of dismay … if his writings on the practice of psychoanalysis are as much about what makes the analyst happy as what might do the patient some good it was because psychoanalysis was a new way, a different way of paying tribute to the most ironic, the most characteristically modern of our wishes: the wish to frustrate ourselves." And yet simultaneously something else always appears to be operating.

The French psychoanalyst Jacques Lacan made considerable play of the seemingly universal phenomenon whereby we have "the compulsion to repeat". For the fan it is more a "compulsion to return", back to that stadium, back to the TV screen. To return to the place of, for example, the nagging toothache. The question is why does our tongue repeatedly flicker back to that same locus of pain? That exquisite moment of dismay?

Lacan covered the more usual explanations: either there is a masochistic insistence, a perverse enjoyment, or there is an attempt to master, to overcome the suffering by a repeated familiarisation. One or the other, or both, will drive us back over and over again. Tottenham played in five FA Cup semi finals during the ten year period from 1991–2001, losing the last four "on the bounce". Was it an in-mixing of these two factors that informed a certain heavy heartedness early on a Sunday morning in April 2001 as our small party yet again headed off to Old Trafford for the match against Arsenal? Lacan (along with psychoanalysis, always sitting in the seat of over-determination), would say "yes and no". For a third element that is of a wilder nature was also present. When our tongue compulsively touches the sore tooth there is also that moment of imaginary belief, the belief in imaginary magic. For it was precisely that which was in play on that morning for us and countless other car loads. The belief that this time, magically, the pain will have vanished! No toothache or, in the case of those Spurs supporters, no rendezvous with crushing disappointment. So perhaps both football and psychoanalysis are inexorably entangled with this crucial element of our being: the magical, the dream space. Forever illusory, but forever spellbinding. The painful so ameliorated by the ecstasy of achievement, the achievement of having successfully slipped the noose of further excruciating anguish, always lying in wait just round the corner.

On a Sunday in May 1998, a few weeks before the World Cup kicked-off in France, a mildly curious gathering of about 120 psychoanalysts, or at least those with an interest or curiosity in psychoanalytic sensibilities, pitched up at Stamford Bridge, the London home of Chelsea Football Club. A meeting of the Psychoanalytic Supporters Club possibly? Well not exactly.

But perhaps not altogether such an odd venue for the psychoanalysts to find themselves in, for those of us who had taken the opportunity to stroll out onto the pitch at lunchtime were confronted by a sight of, what for some, would be an incontestable instance of insanity: at the far end of the ground (the end that used to be affectionately known as "The Shed"), a full scale wedding was taking place. Under the goalposts there were marquees and bouncy castles to the fore, and we learnt that £20,000 had changed hands for the privilege. An instance of "Football Passions" before our very eyes, and indeed this was the title of the conference organised by the Freud Museum (and Barry Richards from the University of East London) that had brought us to Stamford Bridge on that day. Included in the line up were a number of analysts, academics and one or two players. It was this that had drawn, what in conference terms was a perfectly respectable crowd, and let us not forget the football supporter's love of attendance figures, those little details, that component of fetishism, that sustain desire. The purported aim of the event was not so dissimilar to that of this small book: to address the cultural phenomena where "on the eve of the World Cup the level of involvement of millions of people in the drama of football will never have been higher ... the aim of (the conference) is to explore the love of football, its pleasures and frustrations, and the reasons for the game's rise to such prominence." In other words to make some sense of the extraordinary and seemingly near universal popularity of the game of football. And this was to take place through the prism of psychoanalysis; to say something about the psychology of the game.

The French philosopher Jacques Derrida has dubbed the Twentieth Century as "the age of Psychoanalysis". Freud has indeed cast his lengthening shadow over this "psychoanalytic century". By now more will have been written about his life and work than about any other figure in Western history. But might one not simultaneously claim that the last 100 years or so has increasingly become "the age of football", as more and more of us have taken to reading our newspapers backwards. As if it's either "free association" or "association football". For curiously the inauguration of organised football here in England has an approximate parallel trajectory to that of Psychoanalysis. The initial year of the Football League, the precursor to the Premiership, was 1888. And although it was not until 1895, some seven years later, that Freud and Breuer came out with their *Studies on Hysteria*, taken to be the beginnings of psychoanalysis, the bulk of the work for this had been going on at the back end of the 1880s. The aforementioned World Cup, "the greatest and most universal of all sporting competitions" was initially conceived in 1904 at the same time as the establishment of the Federation Internationale de Football Association (FIFA). Although it was not for another quarter of a century before the competition actually took place. Also subject to some delay, the book that is taken to be Freud's most influential achievement, *The Interpretation of Dreams* had been published some four years earlier, in 1900. Actually it came out in November 1899, but the publisher, perhaps having a fondness for round numbers, always chose the date as 1900.

We might even note a curious convergence between "golden eras" as regards psychoanalysis in particular countries and those countries' successes at international football. The obvious parallels are the hey-days of the British Object Relations school (roughly speaking towards the end of the 1950s and early 1960s), and England picking up the World Cup in 1966. In the early 1970s the anti-psychiatrist David Cooper headed off to Buenos Aires, claiming that it was Argentina where "the best psychoanalysis in the world" was currently available. By 1978 Argentina were World Champions. The spread of French psychoanalysis so indelibly associated with the name Lacan was clearly growing throughout the 1970s and 80s, but it was probably not until the 1990s that his "orientation" was so insistently established in media studies and art degree courses across much of Western Europe, not to mention Latin America. At the same time France and its national football team were on the move. Having secured the European Nations Cup by beating Spain in the Final on home soil in 1984, following a semi-final place in the World Cup in Spain two years earlier, they laid the seeds for a future generation of players to gain the ultimate success in 1998.

But back to Stamford Bridge and the conference. It so happened that I was chairing one of the sessions entitled "The players". It was my task to introduce the former West Ham and England player, Trevor Brooking. Now our paths had crossed on a number of other occasions. For example he had refereed a charity match that I had played in at the old Leytonstone ground in Granleigh Road, E17, some years beforehand. Not that I was under any illusion that these moments would have registered for an instance with the urbane Mr Brooking. In this I was not mistaken.

But the instances that I chose to make mention of both involved the European Championships, now colloquially known as, for example, "Euro '96", "Euro 2000". The first was in a small stadium in Düsseldorf, the 1988 championships being held in what was then West Germany. The occasion was a match between the English Press XI and their Dutch counterparts. It was on the morning of the game, to be played later that day, which is forever remembered as "the Van Basten hat trick match". The game in which a somewhat gangly Tony Adams, a fairly recent and raw recruit to the England line-up, was cruelly exposed by the sublime display of the Netherlands centre-forward of that time. I, knowing a few members of the press fraternity following a number of years of stumbling around the Fleet Street Midweek League, had somewhat forlornly gone along to the ground armed with a pair of boots. But my hopes of a game rapidly receded when I saw that about eighteen or nineteen bona fide football writers and the usual sprinkling of ex-professionals had already gathered in the dressing room. However, much to my surprise—not to mention considerable glee—the present-day chairman of the Professional Footballers' Association, Gordon Taylor, was soon to pop his head round the door to call me in. It turned out that a particularly close friend of mine, the *World Soccer* and *Daily Telegraph* writer, Nick Harling, had done a deal: the Press team being short of a keeper, he would go in goal so long as his mate, yours truly, could have a game at right back. And so it turned out that on the balmy June morning in Germany I was lining up alongside the likes of Arsène Wenger (at that time Glenn Hoddle's manager at Monaco), Howard Wilkinson, Brian Talbot, Jim Rosenthal, and of course Trevor Brooking. After about ten minutes, when I actually managed to pass accurately to one of my team mates, I heard the quiet but authoritative words of encouragement ("Good ball") from dear Trevor, and my day was complete.

But it is the second of these fleeting encounters that has more relevance to the matters in hand. For, truth to tell, the initial story is nothing other than an excuse for name-dropping and self-referential indulgences, which is not to suggest that the second is entirely devoid of such nuances. But this time it is 1992 and the venue is now the press centre in Stockholm, "Euro '92" being held in Sweden. Unlike that small stadium in Düsseldorf, now the only people who are allowed access to this centre are those with the appropriate credentials: the much prized press accreditation. At times these centres can feel a little like Fort Knox.

I am standing talking to a long-standing acquaintance from the Wembley press bar, a particularly distinguished football writer and novelist, principally associated with the *Sunday Times*, Brian Glanville. Brooking hove into view. Brian turns and eagerly beckons him over, "Trevor, come and meet one of London's top psychoanalysts" (Glanville having a certain delightful notoriety for excess). All well and good one might think, but I could hardly help but notice a somewhat bemused look; the faint narrowing of the gaze, overcoming Brooking's face. As if to say "If this man is a psychoanalyst, what is he doing standing in our press centre, with (not that he knew this) that falsely acquired press accreditation dangling from his increasingly reddening neck?" "Scamming it" was the answer to this unarticulated question. The moment passed without incident, despite the mild discomfort on my part.

But the point is this. Just as I was an impostor, had no legitimate entitlement to be either on that pitch in Düsseldorf or in the inner sanctum of the press centre in Stockholm adorned with full press credentials, is there not a very real possibility that psychoanalysis, or psychoanalytic sensibilities, by engaging in an interpretative involvement with football is replicating something of the same? In other words, is it not taking up a place of an unentitled intruder, an inappropriate and illegitimate one at that? Does not psychoanalysis always run a considerable and ultimately self-defeating risk of being shown up as fraudulent, as being subject to delusions of grandeur, or at the very least as sounding rather silly whenever it takes upon itself to hold forth on a variety of cultural phenomena? Whenever it strays from the confines, the contract of the consulting room? Whenever there isn't a demand from anyone from anywhere for any psychoanalytic intervention? Although, in defence as it were, Freud once said that "the use of analysis for the treatment of the neuroses is only one of its applications". For him it was a tool of investigation. Thus laying claim to a status as a social analysis, whether between individuals and a concern with relationship, identification and trance, or across generations, involving myth, memory and tradition. But always there is the risk of being a "hanger-on", an irrelevancy, and an irritating one at that.

After all, whilst those trajectories, those of football and psychoanalysis, might have some spurious convergences in terms of the timing of their emergence, it is hardly sustainable that their destinies have followed similar paths. It is not difficult to note an increasing and unrelenting resistance to psycho-analysis, at least in its clinical implications. It is as if, now domesticated and with an almost over-familiarity with regard to its ideas, psychoanalysis can be forgotten, remaindered. As if consigned to the back shelf of the pharmaceutical cupboard, it can be possibly called upon in case of emergency, or when all else has failed. But the prevailing wisdom is that there are a whole host of better things on the market. Clearly its fashionable period, always only very brief, is long gone. In contrast, football, manifestly since that moment in 1990 in Turin of Gazza's tears, has gone from strength to strength, spreading its infectious tentacles wider and wider. We no longer have to read our newspapers backwards, for so much of the time football is on the front page.

Nevertheless it might be possible to claim that precisely because of this uncontrollable contagion of football mania that we are in the presence of some incorrigible sickness. That there is something inherently unhealthy in a world with this over-investment in sport, where football unrelentingly sustains its position as the world's most popular, most ubiquitous game Where a whole range of differing societies are caught up inexorably in a form of uncontainable decadent triviality. Decadent always on the side of romance. Where those infamous words of Bill Shankly, one-time Liverpool manager, renowned, amidst considerable footballing achievements, for celebrating wedding anniversaries by hauling his wife off to reserve team fixtures, that "football is more important than life and death" have come home to roost. So perhaps the time is ripe to call in a psychoanalyst. Perhaps.

However before we go any further it feels important to make some attempt at setting the scene. Football and Psychoanalysis are two utterly discrete genres—areas of specialist knowledge if you will—veering towards two quite distinct cults. When there are two normally very different fields it is inevitable that there are going to be allusions to ideas or people who are commonplace in one but somewhat alien or simply unknown to the other. And as I move between these distinct terrains my voice is going to change, something that happens not merely in this book but also as I move from one world (of grounds, of dressing rooms, of programme fairs, of railway stations and bars) to another (of consulting rooms, of conference halls, of bookshops, of railway stations and bars). Different context, different company, different conversations. Different conversational styles. Hopefully that voice is never other than my own, but there is a very real possibility that in speaking of psychoanalysis it can all go a bit "Merleau Poncy".

Taking my chances, I am going to proceed on the assumption that those who have a familiarity with psychoanalysis are more likely to have a greater awareness of football than the other way round. After all football is a crucial part of our *popular* culture. Or to put it another way that more readers are going to be au fait with the idea of transfer fees, of what it means to be put on the transfer list, than are going to have an immediate grasp of the notion of transference. This is not a bad place to start for it illustrates something of the complexities. On the one hand you have something that is comparatively straightforward: the transferring of a player from one club to another with a fee involved, whilst on the other you have an idea that is far more contentious, far more slippery.

Psychoanalysts come up against an immediate problem when it comes to the term used for the people who come to speak with them: "analysand" feels too arch, "patient" too medical, "client" too . . . I don't quite know what, but it doesn't feel right, so there never seems to be the right word. Football, by and large, has an easier path with those involved, for the most part either being players or fans. But however we call those in analysis, the basic assumption is that they are speaking to their analyst *under transference.* One idea is that this involves a whole host of expectations and assumptions that are transferred from the relations that we had in our past, particularly the early ones with our parents. One of the fundamental ideas about the psychoanalytic relationship is that it is not so much an ordinary relationship, but that it is rather a relationship *about* our relationship with others. And there are virulently opposing schools of thought as to whether this transference, the affective tie that may bind the one who comes for analysis to their analyst for some considerable time, is something that should be referred to or not.

For example the followers of the French psychoanalyst Jacques Lacan see the analyst as a bit like a detective, although not in any straightforward way. This detective is not involved in catching the criminal out, thus solving the crime by clearing away deceit to rendezvous with the truth of the case. Rather the one coming for analysis presumes that there must be someone who will know the truth, and the truth in question is about their desire. "The subject supposed to know" is the Lacanian term for this place that the one coming for analysis puts the analyst in. In other words the analyst is assumed to be an omniscient detective. It is this supposition of knowledge that gives rise to love, and this is where things can get complicated. For whilst there may be quite understandable expectations that the analyst will hand over this assumed knowledge, this expectation is to be refused. Rather the aim is to provoke the one who comes for analysis into becoming detectives in their own case. Clues being provided by the often seemingly trivial details scattered amidst their speech. By and large Lacanian analysts will make no reference or allusions to the relationship between themselves and those who they call the "analysand" . . . the one who is ultimately supposed to being doing the analysis. At times it may look as if they, the analysands, are expected to do all the work, but we must remember that whilst they do it for themselves, they cannot do it *by* themselves.

But there are other schools of thought, particularly the supporters of Melanie Klein. They can appear to want to talk about nothing else than the so called "transference relationship", seemingly bringing about an acute paranoia centred on the analyst. Just to complicate matters others understand this notion of transference as less to do with the particular feelings towards the analyst, but more to do with the light hypnotic state that the psychoanalytic situation provokes; "Trance-ference". Whereby the person who comes for analysis is not so much hypnotised by their analyst, but rather is hypnotised by none other than themselves, and through this gets to hear aspects of what they are saying which otherwise would pass unnoticed. But what rather will be rapidly revealed is that almost any psychoanalytic term will provide a playing field of possibility for heated and at times antagonistic contest.

It is difficult to sustain any analogy; ultimately it will always come up against the cul de sac of impossibility. You just cannot take it any further. But just for a moment allow that the world of psychoanalysis is made up of a large number of clubs—in that sense analogous to football. Rather like the principle clubs in Europe, which we could, for the sake of argument, designate as revolving around a top four or five: for Real Madrid we might cite "Real Melanie Klein" FC. For Manchester United we could have "Jacques Lacan (Dis) United". (Dis-United because there are endless "boardroom" struggles, spites and spasms raging across Paris and beyond, all concerned with the usual story of an ongoing tussle for power and preening rights.) For Bayern Munich the "Object Relations Tradition"; the "Jungians" represented by let us say, Juventus. So on and so forth.

But towering over this is one man who is taken to be the original explorer of unconscious desire, thereby casting him in the position of the ideal analyst, and that man is of course Freud. The football equivalent is possibly not a club side at all, but rather the Brazil national side, particularly the one which won the World Cup in 1970. On second thoughts, it is probably more appropriate to think of these names that play across the psychoanalytic terrain, such as Lacan and Klein, as more akin to international sides—despite being hardly confined to any geographical boundaries. Immediately the Kleinians take on the mantle of Germany, powerful but never very popular. We might extend the analogy to the more insular and pick out certain equivalents that are closer to home—clubs or organisations that are hardly big names on the European or International stage but have a place in the more parochial national leagues. Here in London there is a psychoanalytic organisation called the Guild of Psychotherapists. Solidly mid table, hardly anyone outside the immediate confines of the club would know of their line up, no particular celebrated figures are involved—Charlton Athletic come to mind: perfectly respectable without ever going on to challenge for honours. My own organisation, the Site for Contemporary Psychoanalysis, which is an offshoot from another small scale club, the Philadelphia Association, with an emphasis on an interweave of philosophy and psychoanalysis, might have something of West Ham about them . . . hopefully not the "fade and die" bit, but rather a somewhat "academic" reputation which is never going seriously to disrupt the hegemony of the European giants. The point being that in each country where psychoanalysis is "played" you will find a whole host of competing "clubs" or organisations. All with their own "board of directors", or council of management, all with their playing staff, or list of practitioners, and many will have an "academy", "the juniors", otherwise known as a group of trainees.

Nevertheless, rather akin to football, despite a whole host of differing styles and at times seemingly mutually incompatible traditions, for psychoanalysis is never reducible to "the one", something of the one seems to hold sway. Football is football is football. And the same or something similar goes with psychoanalysis. By and large psychoanalysis offers the therapeutic possibility of sustained self-questioning, the possibility of an examined life. But there are two principle areas that are inevitably involved, that have to be taken seriously. The first is the notion of the Unconscious. Psychoanalytic treatment is predicated on an assumption that there is more to our experience than initially meets the eye. In other words there is always something that we are not as yet aware of. Various aspects of our lives escape our conscious control, and by a focusing on what is actually said we may, at times reluctantly, acknowledge that we find ourselves saying more than we meant to say. It has become pretty commonplace. After all the term a "Freudian slip" is hardly an instance of "talking shop". Dreams, jokes and slips of the tongue are instances whereby we may glimpse something of these unconscious processes that inform us all. Psychoanalysts seem especially fond of dreams, which long before Freud were taken to be sources of knowledge. Often linked to predicting a future, but often if not invariably calling for some expert who would decipher or decode a particular dream. But something of this changed with Freud. They were still understood to be curious sources of knowledge, but often now more concerned with our past. And the messages were not necessarily welcome, bringing to the fore aspects of ourselves that we might have little desire to acknowledge: murderous and sexual aspects. From that moment it became increasingly difficult to sustain the idea that we are entirely masters in our own house. Rather we emerged as divided: conflicted between what we were conscious of wanting and those less appealing and in part unconscious longings.

The second thing that is crucial is sexuality. Sexuality, less as having some fixed point of origin or more or less stable objectives, but something that can drive us into sensuous desirous relationships not only with other people but, for example, into the arms of football. It can be said that the "Freudian subject", which in some historical sense now we all are, has this idea of him or herself as being a "subject of desire". As if there is only one sort of truth about us: the truth—or the puzzle—of the complexities of our desire. And that truth is sexual. And part of this puzzle is that it seems as if this desire can go too far. Where pleasure converges on pain, where we come up against an unbearably excessive pleasure that starts to look a lot like anguish. Freud called this "beyond the pleasure principle". The followers of Lacan use the term "jouissance", which is also

French for cum. Football fans have a variety of terms for it but it congeals around the anxiety of "getting gubbed again". More crudely put: "getting fucked over" or "stuffed", sustaining the psychoanalytic assumption that this desire will always have something of the sexual entangled with it.

For those readers amongst you that find that there is a tendency to glaze over when the subject matter starts to get more psychoanalytical than you have appetite for, may I suggest that you treat it a bit like the increasingly truncated close season. Just be patient and before you know it, it's football time again.

Parklife

The general anaesthetic gently clearing, allowing the world to gradually come back into focus, finds me lying in a hospital bed at the Royal Free Hospital in North London. A softly spoken registrar is explaining what has been done to my knee. I had snapped my anterior cruciate ligament ten minutes from the end of a veterans game at the Corinthian Casuals ground out at Tolworth. I was forty-eight. Whilst having a vague awareness that on the road to our actual death we are all subject to a seriality of "other deaths", in that something that once was no longer exists (our childhood, a love tie, a student life, a particular job are just a few examples), nevertheless each and every encounter with the realisation that something is over, finished, kaput, will always be something of a trauma. Invariably it will have come too soon. And this was no exception. Somewhat tentatively I enquired, "Er . . . chances of playing again?" The answer was emphatic, "No, never! Not even a kick about in the back garden."

What was revealed in that moment was the doctor's intuitive understanding of the compulsive quality, akin to the sexual itch, that underscores our need for play. That seemingly barely

containable eagerness, the St Vitus's dance moment of exuberance, as soon as a ball comes into view. To juggle, to tap, to
caress, the enjoyment entangled in the elasticity of control as
momentarily it comes to rest under the ball of our foot. Always
a love affair. In that moment forever cancelled, extinguished,
ruptured, gone for good.

There has to be a place for denial in our panoply of defences.
For sometimes it is possible to get away with it. And it wasn't
that I had not tried. When the injury happened it had indeed been
excruciating, but blithely I had assured my team mates of my
availability for next week's game. For six weeks I had hobbled
around with a horribly swollen knee, which periodically would
seize up in some agonising spasm. I was reminded of those
moments depicted in comics from one's childhood where pain
would be illustrated by a huge globule of sweat spontaneously
bursting forth from someone's forehead. That is what it was like,
but the forehead was entirely mine.

I struggled on, trying to convince myself that eventually,
magically, all would be well. Until one night in Paris, in the
context of one of those weekends away, so saturated with little
pleasures. I had slipped away from our small party in order to
feed the addiction, heading up to the north of the city for Red
Star's early evening game. All was fine until I turned from my
seat in the main stand to leave at the final whistle. In that moment
once again my knee locked in a torturous seizure. I couldn't
move. Others, utterly unaware of my predicament, understandably brushed past me and off into the night, leaving me
increasingly frantic as one by one the floodlight pylons were
switched off in the now deserted stadium. I knew that I had to
get out or I could be there until early Monday morning, this being
some time before the ubiquity of the mobile phone. Somehow,
through gritted teeth, I managed to slowly haul myself up to the
top of the stand to locate a small cluster of schoolboys engaged
in a desultory kick about down below. In my faltering French I

managed to catch their attention, and to my eternal gratitude, quite literally, they came to my rescue, sympathetically support- ing my gradual, stumbling exit from the St Ouen ground. Taking forever to crawl to the metro it was only through further sympathetic awareness of one of those delightful dark eyed Parisian gamines, who seeing that I was now trapped in the seat in the carriage, for the slightest movement would set off another spiral of agony, somehow managed to "shoulder" me up the stairs and out into the square where the sanctuary of my hotel beckoned. The next day spent morosely sipping coffees at Sartre's old haunt "Les Deux Magots" I resolved that first thing Monday morning I would present myself at the local A&E (although six weeks after the event hardly constituted "an emergency"), and within twenty-four hours I was under that anaesthetic.

It is stating the obvious that most interest in—and indeed most writing about football—invariably concentrates on the profes- sional game. Even within that tendency there is an inevitable preoccupation with the more successful end of the spectrum. Whether it be the famous teams and players and the international tournaments such as the World Cup, European Nations, Copa America and suchlike, or closer to home and the dark hole of the Premiership, the pit from which the mania leaps forth.

But, as does all our interest, this stems from the ordinary, indeed the simple activity of playing: of playing football. How many of my generation began their involvement by kicking a ball against a wall, progressing to the local recreation ground for a kick-about with the legendary little heaps of discarded clothing operating as goalposts. Archived away will be those moments of indulgent grandparents dipping into bottomless purses to replace yet another busted "Frido", consigned to the dustbin after fruitless attempts over the stove with the allegedly magical repair tong to reseal its fragile, plasticy surface. For previous generations, certainly in inner cities, battered tennis balls and goal posts erratically chalked on tenement walls were so often the order of the day. The obsessive alchemy accompanied by John Bull bicycle repair kits attending to punctured bladders. Such memories are embedded in so many ordinary lives. Nowadays it is more often children being taken in cars by enthusiastic parents for the Saturday morning game. Sometimes those same parents stumbling out on a bleary eyed, faintly alcohol soaked Sunday morning in pathetic attempts to squeeze yet another drop from the inexhaustible well of football enjoyment. I say pathetic, not in some sneering, condescending way, nor is it envy, however much I would so love still to be out there myself, but rather that all our strivings, our personal concerns are ultimately pathetic when set in the context of the greater scheme of things. But pathetic or not, nostalgia has its pleasures.

However it is almost impossible to orientate ourselves amidst all the variations of how any of us might enter this terrain. Whether it be spontaneous or induced, with an attendant hyper-awareness or all suffused by a mild daze. Sometimes our own affair, sometimes our parent's. There can be no suggestion that it will be the same in Surbiton as it will in Soweto; whilst there will be a universal invariant with regard to the game itself, there will also be a corresponding universal variation as each culture, each epoch, each continent will emphasise one aspect to the possible detriment of others. The invariant with regard to the inauguration of football in anyone's life is variation, diversity.

But the point of all this is to draw attention to the fact that, almost without exception, anyone who has even a passing interest in the game will at some point or other in their lives have played, will have tapped a ball around in some shape or form, somehow, somewhere. In other words they will know something of the enjoyment that playing football offers, and in its way an offer of an enjoyment in the pleasures of recall, as if nostalgia is at the heart of the project. Part of the exquisite joy being the prospect of the almost Wordsworthian "recollection(s) in tranquillity" of ecstatic or triumphant moments. "Store up the memories for nothing lasts." Some goals, as they say, just live in the memory. But this of course will be the case for all sports: anyone who has played cricket will have a potential repertoire of memories of the "sweet spot" or a particularly "blinding" catch.

Although it may not, at times, appear quite like that, it is this issue of enjoyment that is the principal concern of psychoanalysis. But this needs considerable clarification, because enjoyment is not to be simply conflated with pleasure, or indeed with joy. Possibly one of the most important things that Freud drew attention to was that so often what we are so insistently caught up in, that we return to over and over again, are compelled to repeat as it were, is not necessarily pleasurable. Watching Rochdale on a regular basis comes to mind, although why I should pick on poor Rochdale in all probability will elude both me and my analyst. We don't have any equivalent for the French word "jouissance", with its link to sexual fluids and legal possession, so frequently translated as "enjoyment", and it seems to me that we could do with one. Curiously I am told that the French do not have our word "fun" in their vocabulary. Not that this will do for this term "jouissance". Similarly there is too much "joy" in the word "enjoyment", there is too much on the side of pleasure. But the trouble is that we do not have a better one, and "jouissance" feels, well . . . a little too French. The word seems to engage in an in-mixing of the words "jouer", to play, and "sens", or sense in the sense of meaning, meaningful. So we can see that something that is "in play" or "plays" or drives us whilst being simultaneously meaningful to us, can be crucially linked to what we, having no other term, might call our "enjoyment". Even if it is not especially enjoyable. At times it looks as if what we have opted for is downright frustrating. For so many football seems caught up in precisely this. In other words something returns us to it over and over again in an intensely agonising insistence: it is the form or one of the forms of our enjoyment. An enjoyment that is informed by a certain madness. This has a special quality, a quality that by its very nature will be impossible to pin down, to define.

We may note that whatever form it takes play is always already more than mere physiological reflex or psychological release. It has always a significant function. In other words there is some sense to it. In play there is something "at play" which goes beyond the immediate needs of life, and simultaneously gives meaning to the action. Whatever principles we might come to see as essential to play we cannot fall back on ideas of the instinctual. If not least because it would be a monstrous betrayal of Freud's initiatives to think of our being as organised in advance by "the Laws of Nature". Psychoanalysis proposes an absolute rupture as far as we, human beings, are concerned from the automatic and immediate "natural" or instinctual play of, let us say, a cat. Even though football, like cats and mating, has its seasons.

Yet in so many ways animals play just like us. We only have to watch cats to see that certain essentials of human play are present in their frolicking. They invite one another to play by a certain ceremoniousness of attitude and gesturing. Almost as if they exchange pennants and handshakes, somewhat warily, before the game begins. They also appear to abide by certain rules of the game, such as you do not bite (or at least not bite too hard), and they seem to perform pretending to be very angry. But crucially, and most importantly, it is safe to say that they are having enormous fun and enjoyment. We may note that the capacity for laughter and for smiling is exclusively human, whilst the significant function of play is common to both animals and mankind. If they could, we can only assume the cats would be smiling, laughing even, at the end of their playing together. More rarely would it deteriorate into some form of "going off in the tunnel" at the end of their game. Clearly animals play so they must be more than merely mechanical. We play and we know that we play, and so we are more than rational beings. To the extent that play is always beyond rationality, is beyond meaning, it is on the side of the transgressive. And yet it is in and of itself; it is for its own sake.

But let us return to our playing. Of course it will have a physiological or biological substratum (show me a human activity that evades this) but it will always be culturally moulded, always returning us to the undecidability of the infinite opposition of nurture and nature. What is essentially true for football will in all probability operate for all sports, but possibly what goes a little way towards differentiating football is a basic simplicity. You don't even have to get changed to play: jackets will suffice for goal posts, not even footwear is necessary in some continents, so no call for expensive kit, nor any real need for elaborate coaching. The exhilaration and enjoyment, the same essential structures will saturate the situation whether it is an impromptu kick about in a park, on a beach, wherever, as will be generated by the World Cup Final itself with 80,000 spectators urging the teams on in an architecturally state-of-the-art stadium.

The fundamental requirements are so very simple, basic even: a ball and some space. "The goal shall consist of two upright posts, eight yards apart (inside measurement), joined by a horizontal crossbar the lower edge of which shall be eight feet from the ground". That is what the FIFA rules lay down. But what actual players do, all across the world, from the rural expanses of the African subcontinent to the cramped housing estates of the post industrial European hinterland, is actually quite different, as my mother was to learn on returning from a particular family holiday one summer evening. Much to her horror, she was confronted by a thin strip of wood that had been nailed to two adjacent trees in our front garden, at a height impeccably conforming to the aforementioned FIFA regulations. Whilst we had been away an enterprising mate of the "sod the daffodils" school of thought had set to and made some "ground improve-ments" during the "close season". Sadly this did not make into Neville Gabie's exquisite book of photographs *Posts*, but the principle was the same. What players do the world over is, of course, improvise.

For some, cricket too will quickly come to mind, but already the complications are multiplied, indeed doubled, for you not only need a ball but inevitably a bat, however inventive the construction of a wicket. Gabie states the obvious when he patiently points out that goal posts are far from all white, measured and set within immaculately tended pitches. And yet, as testimony to the universality of the game and this capacity to improvise, they are instantly recognisable wherever you go in the world. They are an inherently familiar part of so many varied landscapes. Gabie, at heart a sculptor, began to recognise how the posts mirrored the environment that they were in. "Where there was no wood to hand, stones, string, metal, chalk or paint could be used. And without a field in which to play, a garage door, a street corner or a car park became reasonable substitutes." Somehow what he picked up on—exemplified in his collection of exquisite photographs—is that the posts inscribe a "place", a site of potentiality, for dreams and fantasies, and above all, for delirious play.

Certain inherent properties of the game (essentially that of struggle—but then that will be true of all sport), provide the backdrop for a multiplicity of possibilities for a whole range of different personalities to express themselves. Rugby, as an example, appears blunted in comparison; allowing for a desperate oversimplification, principally two possibilities appear to insist: either one enrols as a hulking, bullying, brutish member of the "pack", or alternatively, a fleet footed, jinking three quarter. Football in contrast offers so many variations for self expression, and so has many possibilities for revealing something of some-body's character, and an infinite opportunity to relish these differences. These possibilities are there every bit as much up at the recreation ground or in the five-a-side gym as in the Premier League, with its undersoil, over-heated and over-hyped game.

But let us examine some ideas about playing itself. Of course there have been lots of ideas with regard to the nature and the significance of play, all in an attempt to assign it a particular position in the scheme of things. By and large its utility is taken for granted but its point—the answer to the question "what is it for?"—clearly varies. You might think that it would have something to do with "a discharge of superabundant vital energy", an outlet for "harmful influences". Or in more ordinary language: aggression. If so, you might have been as taken aback as I was one Saturday afternoon behind the main stand at Scarborough. On my way in search of the half time cuppa I was roughly apprehended by the local constabulary and told in no uncertain terms that any further swearing on my part (I had taken a particular dislike to, in my not so considered opinion, a rather inadequate linesman) would result in "immediate ejection". And there I was, blithely assuming that, for many of us, it was these "discharges" that was precisely what we, the fraternity of the faithful, had gathered together for.

Other theorising has it that play enables us to satisfy an imitative instinct or simply to gratify a need for relaxation. For some it is a way in which we prepare ourselves for the more serious "work" of life. That via role-playing we gain an education. It is part of a learning process, possibly to learn the necessary restraint that we all may need. Others will emphasise the call to exercise an innate desire to compete and to dominate. But whatever the ideas, there is one basic assumption which is that play has to serve something other than play itself.

Certainly my playing football (principally in the Greater London area, only occasionally straying outside the confines of the M25), provided a side effect as it were: an almost limitless opportunity to explore the "London that nobody knows", to filch from the title of one of the many books of essays and illustrations from that marvellous pen and ink flaneur Geoffrey Fletcher. Ranging from East Acton playing fields, Albert Road

Rec, Palewell Common and on to the more evocatively named "Hare and Hounds", "Spotted Dog", "Dog Kennel Hill", via the Guinness brewery grounds out at Park Royal, only faintly scratching the surface of literally hundreds of grounds that I played on over the years, all permitting those small, exquisitely pleasurable geographical meanderings.

It is one of the great theorists with regard to play, Johan Huizinga, who drew attention to there being something lacking in all these explanations. "As a rule they leave the primary quality of play, as such, virtually untouched" he claimed in his masterly *Homo Ludens* published in 1949. Why is a huge crowd roused to frenzy by a football match is indeed one of his very questions. For Huizinga it was the intensity, the absorption, *"the power of maddening"* (my emphasis), that was linked to the very essence of play itself. He wanted to recuperate the fun in playing, to emphatically emphasise that "it is the fun-element that characterises the essence of play." It is he who drew attention to the fact that no other modern language has the exact equivalent to this word fun. I am reminded of an occasion during the Copa America, in 1999, when it was held in Paraguay; a group of us had headed off to see the Iguaçu Falls, and we came upon a platform jutting out into the spray. Almost all of the tourists, including myself, held back, concerned about getting drenched. All apart from three of my friends, one of whom on returning, completely saturated from head to toe, smilingly muttered "Only the English . . ."

Huizinga wants to suggest that all the other, perfectly valid aspects of play are ultimately secondary, subservient to this foundational characteristic. His claim is that this essential aspect, fun, is beyond analysis; it "resists all logical interpretation". We might recall that Freud eventually conceded that there is something about us all that will insist, will resist if you will, all attempts at analysis. Somehow play is different from ordinary life, and it is this special form of activity (in this instance football), as a "significant form", as a social function that is our subject. For the sake of the argument there will always be a convergence between playing and watching football. Like so many of us, the poet and writer, and editor of *The Faber Book of Soccer*, Ian Hamilton would have preferred to have been a footballer. When he was asked what he was like at playing, he came up with this classic response, "a bit knackered . . . but you should see me *watch* it". But we will get back to that. As we will to Huizinga, who's *Homo Ludens* was described by a fellow consummate theorist of play, Roger Caillois, as "the most important work in the philosophy of history in our century".

It was Caillois in *Les Jeux et les Hommes* who proposed a fourfold classification of games: games of mimesis or expression, games of competition, games of chance, and perhaps most interestingly, games of giddiness, of the whirl. It does not take long to see that football engages in all of these four potentialities. Clearly part of the fun of playing football (and watching for that matter) are the exciting opportunities for self-expression and mimicking. Play certainly allows both the most impulsive and aggressive of us and simultaneously the more inhibited and conventional to be on the same pitch (or high up behind the goal). It is as possible to satisfy a concern with avoiding humiliation as the defender or the spoiling midfield player. The notion that goalkeepers are somehow different always exists, because although their aim is to prevent, to protect, somehow humiliation is always, spectacularly, just round the corner. But simultaneously for the creative midfield player, for the flying "tanner ball" winger, and incorrigibly linked to the glory of the player who puts the ball in the net, football is an excellent medium for exhibitionism. Otherwise known as exuberant showing off, being flash. For many it will be possible to oscillate between these two states, for almost all can partake of the golden opportunity to be highly aggressive, to engage in the domination of another to the point of bullying, but always within a highly structured, accepted set of rules. A team game that allows for a peculiar selfishness that at times, if David Ginola's dribbling was anything to go by, can border on the pathological, seems to have something for everyone. And of course pathology is no deterrent to becoming an extraordinarily good player. We only have to have the vaguest knowledge of football to know that it is not just for their footballing abilities that the likes of George Best, Eric Cantona, Paul Gascoigne and Diego Maradona are so celebrated. Indeed for so many, spectacular failure in the classroom has absolutely no bearing on success out on the park.

A lot of this is to do with there being no right way to play football. This is not to say that practice and a capacity to master certain basics like trapping the ball or passing accurately are not fundamental. Despite an apparent contagion, certainly in the Premiership, of crosses finding the first (as in nearest), defender, most professional footballers have spent most of their childhoods doing virtually nothing else. But in contrast to sports such as tennis, cricket, or golf—where avoiding mistakes takes on a much higher priority—football is constantly a vehicle for the surprise element, for the creative, the imaginative. It is often the more celebrated player (such as Matt Le Tissier or Chris Waddle for example), who will be the one who is the greatest risk-taker, the one most likely to fly off at a tangent, rather than the one who compulsively thinks of defence, of minimising risk. It is inscribed in the language of the game: great goal scorers are those who are the best "taker of chances". In other words are "chancers". Waddle was quite explicit when interviewed during the 1990 World Cup "We've got to have licence. They don't say to Baggio or Hagi or Gullit, we want you back defending. They don't say to Voller or Littbarski or Klinsmann or Scifo, you can't run about, stick in your zone. They go where they want, they make options." Options, so many options. Perhaps this has something to do with why football is, back to that word, so much *fun* to play.

Yet why is it so popular to watch, and obviously not just "live", at the game, but principally, as Sky TV will testify, on our television screens? Indeed at the World Cup in Germany it was possible to witness a comparatively new phenomenon: countless people travelling considerable distances with no thought of, seemingly with little desire of actually going to a game, but rather to gather in large numbers to gaze at giant screens. It would be foolish to think that identification does not play a part somewhere along the line. As I have said, there is hardly anybody who is watching a game who has not played at some level or other. Even for those who were humiliatingly always last to be picked for the teams during P.E. lessons may often develop a passion for supporting their team. Now they have access to a sport that once barely included them. For others, indeed for most of us, there is the possible identification with those who can play far better than we ever could, who can do the "impossible" things that were always beyond us, and all is entangled with the prevailing tendency to live our lives via fictive narratives. Football as soap opera, or more accurately docu-soap. We have some access (but only some), to what goes on in the dressing room, (Beckham and the flying boot), out at the training ground (Hartson and the flying kick), or in hotel bedrooms with other players' wives (Cantona and his departure from Leeds United) but, and this is Ian Hamilton again, "What we all really want is what all spectators want . . . more access." But there again, possibly not. Precisely because such narratives are behind the scenes, veiled in some way, is what may go a considerable way to sustaining our fascination and our desire.

The press and TV provide us, and of course football is not alone in this, with a whole host of possible sites of identification. We are drawn to individuals whom we like to see something of ourselves in, or something that we aspire to. As a teenager at the back end of the fifties the player that I identified with the most, wanted to be the most, was the diminutive ball player from

Tottenham, Tommy Harmer. He was slight, and with typical adolescent self-consciousness I had myself down as being particularly puny. Neither did he appear to be blessed with any great speed and, as anyone who has ever played with me will bear witness, that was hardly a particular asset of mine. But what he could do, with seemingly effortless trickery, was slip and slide, graciously glide round much bigger, tougher, rougher looking players, all out to take the ball off him with crunching tackles. He seemed almost cerebral by comparison to almost all of his contemporaries. I was hooked, endlessly seeking to emulate him with intricate dribbles round the back garden, school playgrounds and assorted recreation grounds. To little avail. Then again we pick out or pick on others whom we loathe (apologies to Paul "Ollie" Allen) in all probability, as psychoanalysis would suggest, because we unconsciously recognise some disavowed aspect of ourselves. In other words they too are rather like us. So we are drawn to live vicariously, live by proxy as it were, when we gaze so intently at our heroes or demonise our villains.

Psychoanalysis has always had a considerable interest in play. One man, the British analyst Donald Winnicott, pretty much made playing his hallmark, his particular calling card, his signature tune. He insisted on underlining psychoanalysis, psychotherapy, call it what you will, as a form of playing: "it has to do with two people playing together" he said in his hugely influential work *Playing and Reality*. Of course he is not thinking of play in terms of an organised game such as football, yet something of this play spirit will endure. Intriguingly he appeared to have a distrust (or some form of dismay) when it came to excitement, and yet it is difficult to think of football without acknowledging that it can be, ought to be, an intensely exciting form of playing, and at the same time an immensely exciting form of play to watch. It's as if we never quite know what to do with excitement. Our initial experiences of it will be bodily, physical excitement, so often linked with our little feet, with kicking out.

But also of course with our mouth, our lips, sucking and biting. Winnicott suggested that what he called our "instinctual life" always gave rise to a conflict, to considerable concern for us all. On the one hand we value the idea of freedom that is suffused with the idea of freedom of expression, of instinctual expression. But simultaneously we may be afraid, terrified even of the effects of such expression. Its potential destructiveness. So much so that we become desperate to be subject to some form of control. Thus the necessity that our games have rules, the need for referees. Such fears and the call for some form of containment, so emblematic of paranoia, may be negotiated either by insisting on being in control oneself, by lording it over others, or by being controlled through continuously handing over responsibility to an idealised leader. Winnicott could see that either of these possibilities could get seriously out of hand, resulting in an impoverishment of someone's spontaneity and desire; a diminution of the capacity to play that he held to be so essential to our being.

Sometimes it feels as if psychoanalysis can get in a bit of a muddle over excitement, so often lodging it under the sign of mania. A solid stream of thought appears to head off only too readily in the following direction: excitable now becomes co-terminus with the hyper-manic, as a defence against, a sort of being on the run from something other, something more valuable, something like sadness or mourning. At times it feels as if Winnicott wants to emphasise a little too much the freedom that comes from a freedom *from* the tyranny of bodily excitement, thereby allowing a more meditative absorption. So exemplified by the child engrossed in play. In contrast the freedom *to* hurl oneself into a frenzy of appetite and desire feels denigrated, downplayed. To throw oneself at the cross pinging across the penalty box, to obey the call, to allow the possession that simultaneously curses, to be overwhelmed by the heat and dazzle of football can feel almost frowned upon. The freedom to be deranged. The freedom to lock on.

And yet I may be being unfair to this particular psychoanalyst, who at times has an almost Bobby Moore status and reputation in the profession, the subject of compulsive idealisation. For at times, just as Moore's immaculate performance in the heat of Guadalajara in the 1970 World Cup allows us to understand why, so certain of Winnicott's initiatives reveal why all who have an interest in psychoanalysis should be so resoundingly grateful to the man. Even if he was, in part, rather on the run from the excitement of the erotic. Nevertheless what he saw quite clearly is that any attempt to create a formalised standard for how we should live our lives could only open up a potential vista of unrelenting compliance. The net result whereby all would meekly submit to psychoanalysis as an oppressive "mummy knows best" routine, could only end up inhibiting, pathologising, prohibiting even, the ordinary pleasures in life.

This is what he had to say about football. Well he never actually wrote about football at all, not one word. You do not on the whole find many psychoanalysts who do. This is about an example from the era of the music hall, but it might just as well be about football. And so, playfully, I am going to proceed on that basis . . . "For instance, one is at a football ground and onto the pitch come the players, trained to liveliness. One can say that here is the primal scene, here is exhibitionism, here is anal control, here is masochistic submission to discipline, here is the defiance of the super-ego (otherwise known as instructions from the dug-out). Sooner or later one adds: here is LIFE. Might it not be that the main point of the performance is a denial of deadness, a defence against depressive 'death inside' ideas, the sexualization being secondary." (*The Manic Defence* in *Through Paediatrics to Psycho-Analysis*).

It is Adam Phillips in his excellent introductory book on Winnicott who underlines that performance, and the fun and excitement so associated with it (thus implicating football), has value precisely because it is a denial, a defence even, against deadness. There has to be room for a differentiation between the inappropriate "manic defence" and "normal (or ordinary) reassurance through reality". The reality of transporting, intoxicating excitement.

Probably, at least within psychoanalytic circles, Winnicott is especially known for his ideas about transitional space. The term "transitional object" has become as lodged within psychoanalytic conversations at least in Britain, as say, "the back four" has in football parlance. We have yet to develop the idea that a number of terms so emblematic of psychoanalysis such as transference, transformation, and transitional are underpinned by ideas of trance. That particular arena of experience that is so indubitably linked to being seduced, transported, mesmerised, and enchanted. All converging on ideas of being hypnotised, of being possessed. As has been mentioned before it is so often a woman, going to a game for the first time, who will draw attention to it: that within a certain radius of the ground for an hour or more before the kick off you can hardly fail to note a particular purposefulness of gait, an unwavering glaze in the eye, a sense of unalterable preoccupation. Those tell-tale signs so articulated in that famous Lowry painting *"Going to the Match"* that now adorns the office of the Professional Footballers Association here in England. Hypnotism on legs.

The sort of things that Winnicott meant by "transitional object" were those peculiarly precious items that almost all of us as children just had to have with us as we went off to sleep. Later in life a substitute in the shape of the glass of whiskey or the indulgence in a spliff may well come into being. This precious bit of cloth—or whatever it is—has tremendous value because it enables, facilitates as Winnicott would have it, the transition from being awake to going off to sleep. These ideas have led many an analyst to ceaselessly ask the question, not so much "who am I?" for the patient, as in parent figure, sibling, or lover, but rather "what use am I being put to?" That is why the technical term "object relations school" to denote a particular psychoanalytical "gang" or grouping has always seemed so clumsy. More pertinently we have objectives rather than "objects".

And the question that we must not stray from is what objective (or objectives) does football serve? Where does it take so many of us? To return to a transitional or trance-itional space, that's where. Of course at times it must seem that an over investment in football is so utterly adolescent, and there is something to this, but in a good sense: adolescence always on the side of the in-between, on the side of the transitional, on the side of a rite of passage.

Of course it would be absurd to suggest that only football can do this. Winnicott was quite explicit about this: in our adult life both art and religion are instances of access to this sort of thing, and above all: music. He saw this form of space to which a child will so tenaciously cling, and where we as adults may find ourselves thinking, although probably less likely to articulate for fear of appearing stupid, as "an intermediate area of experiencing to which inner reality and external life both contribute". A space that mediates between fantasy and what is really going on. Such space operates, according to Winnicott in *Through Paediatrics to Psycho-analysis*, as "a resting place for the individual engaged in the perpetual task of keeping inner and outer reality separate yet inter-related."

What happens with football when it comes to supporting a particular team is so often an instance of these transitional spaces. How often do we cling assiduously to the idea, the fantasy, that by some magical act we can influence the course of a game? In all probability a rather unsubtle defence against the excruciatingly frustrating recognition that in fact we are utterly helpless when it comes to influencing any moment of a match, far less the eventual outcome. For years whenever Tottenham conceded a corner I would utter a mantra, conspicuous by its unoriginality. Starting when I was about fifteen with a barely audibly muttered

"Keep'em out Hovis" (a reference to Bill Brown—work it out!) and on via Pat Jennings, Barry Daines, even "Bunter" Kendall and on to the more recent incumbents of the goalkeeper's jersey such as Ray Clemence, Eric Thorstvedt and Ian Walker. This was done with the sublime conviction that unless I performed this ritual we would surely let in a goal. Now it is quite clear that in over forty years of watching quite a lot of my team there has to have been an occasion that an opponent scored following a corner. But I have no recollection of this. As clear an instance of repression as you will find; repression insistently linked to trauma. I always promised myself that I would abandon this particular psychic tic once it had stopped working its magic. But what happened was that I decided (and I shall happily admit that it was only a couple of seasons ago), that in all honesty, it was quite unnecessary. It was a little private lunacy. Whether I uttered these words or not was not going to make the slightest difference to the outcome of a particular corner kick. But, privately of course, I could not help but notice how reluctant I was to let go of this, as if the catastrophe of conceding a goal would automatically follow. In a similar way for many years, but only ever acknowledged to myself, I was secretly convinced that if I had not been at a game then it, the game itself, would have somehow been different. Not in a simple cause and effect way—where if I go we win, if I am absent we lose, that sort of thing—merely that it would have been different. As if my pathetic presence or absence, amidst a crowd of 35,000 or so, would in some way have some influence on the proceedings, Clinging to such ideas, however privately, however crazily, is analogous to our holding on, for dear life as it were, to that special bit of cloth in order to fend off our dismay at our irretrievable helplessness in the face of the sheer randomness of life. Trace elements of omnipotent longings.

But let us return to the idea of football as play. To resume the thesis that football is one of the ways in which it has been possible to retain elements of the "play forms", of the innocence so associated with childhood. Of course psychoanalysis would seek to problematise any such notions of the "innocence of childhood". Nevertheless the spontaneous delight in "innocently" tapping a ball around in a park, accompanied by enthusiastic shouts of "put it on me bonce" would seem to suggest that some umbilical link to our childhood is sustained. But to what extent does such spirit genuinely pervade our lives? Superficially it might seem that sport, and in particular football, has more than compensated for any loss of play forms in our contemporary world. Football installs yet another place of ritual, of fun and festivity in our lives. And this is whether it be "when Saturday comes" and out come the boots, or the more casual but insistent quickening of the pulse when it is that time when our TVs are saturated with World Cup coverage.

Historically for a complexity of reasons, but in part informed by the church, there was an underestimation of the significance of the body. Christian ideals so often left little room for any organised practice of sport or cultivation of bodily exercise. Never mind the issue of the sensual. This was partly rectified by the Victorian public school ethos, so saturated by "muscular Christianity" (written up in *Tom Brown's Schooldays*), underpinned by the "healthy body leads to a healthy mind" mantra, not to mention the promotion of the "fit boy" to satisfy the predilections of the Christian Brothers in Ireland. But it is possible to note a gradual transition from occasional amusement, although it is rather difficult to imagine Dr Johnson and Boswell, just as an example, setting off for a jog, to the modern day system of organised clubs and matches. The shift from collective mayhem to the formation of sides or groups playing against each other, whether it be village against village, school against school, or one part of the town against another. Huizinga's claim is that England "became the cradle and focus of modern sporting life", in part as an effect of the ubiquity of common land and the flatness of the terrain lending itself to much of the nation becoming a "playing" field.

Accompanying these developments were the establishment of strict rules and a keeping of records. But is it possible, inevitable even, that with an increased systemisation and regimentation of football that something of the pure "play quality" begins to recede? We may notice that in England the old distinction between amateur and professional has long gone; the last FA Amateur Cup competition being held in 1974.

It is over twenty years or more since Keith Burkinshaw paused on his way out of White Hart Lane to turn and gaze wistfully at the club that he had served with considerable distinction as manager. His decision to move on had been informed by the increasing growth of corporate influence at Tottenham Hotspur. Legend has it that he uttered a phrase that continues to resonate to this day. It is embedded in the lore of English football, but actually what happened was that as he turned for one further glance, Ken Jones, the football writer, who was walking alongside him, told him the story of Ebbetts Field, the past home of the Brooklyn Dodgers. Wrecking balls saw to the caving in of the walls of an ancient, much loved stadium and Frank Sinatra had captured the mood in his inimitable style when he sang "There used to be a ball club over there." Apparently Burkinshaw nodded, and whilst Tottenham's ground was not about to be reduced to landfill the sentiment was similar: "There used to be a football club over there" has now passed into football folklore. Nothing prevents the thought that Burkinshaw was in the forefront of those who had a sense that football was moving away from the people; it had begun to lose its "innocence". He confided in Jones that "where the team was all, the centre of everything that went on at a football club, it has become just a part of a marketing formula."

By now money dominates the scene and so many of us have utterly lost touch with the way that football is now being run.

What does the average fan know—or care—about plcs, share dealings, the profit motive set against the performance of the team? It is as if there are two entirely conflicting trains of thought: the supporters continue to dream of progress "out on the park" whilst the directors concern themselves with minimising losses and, if possible, some measure of financial stability. Not to mention considerable lining of their own pockets. Football now involves both serious but simultaneously crazy sums of money. Each week newspapers are full of disturbing facts that seep out of football's woodwork. Salaries that are out of all sensible proportion to revenue (and we are not talking merely about the players), tales of gross financial indiscretions, of profligate management, the culture of brown paper "bungs" exchanging hands in hotel toilets, all invariably with barely a glance in the direction of the feelings of the supporters. Hardly surprising that the sports pages are juxtaposed with the financial section in so many newspapers, for over half the "stories" appear to be about money, whether it be about salaries demanded (thanks to Ruud Gullit the word "netto" entered our vocabulary), transfer fees, the pending downturn in television revenue, calamitous debts and insistent calls for the need for prudence. All seem to illustrate that football, even at its highest professional level, will always be in danger of losing its way once it forgets that it is primarily a game, not principally a corporate enterprise.

There once was an era in England when there was a maximum dividend of seven per cent imposed on all club directors, who were invariably the principle shareholders. It is not that this period in the history of the game was some rose-tinted ideal but one thing that is for sure is that the chairmen of football clubs were by and large anonymous figures. So they should have been, according to the sublime Len Shackleton (of Bradford Park Avenue, Newcastle and Sunderland fame) who, when he turned to "What Chairmen know about Football" in his book *Clown Prince of Soccer*, left a couple of pages blank. So anonymous by and large, unless they held high administrative office within the Football Association or were involved in some comparatively high level scandal. During that time it was probably true that many people knew that comedians such as Tommy Trinder was chairman of Fulham, that Eric Morecombe was on the board at Luton Town, or that certain families held controlling interests at a number of First Division clubs. But hardly anyone gave them a second thought. Today, people such as Abramovich at Chelsea or the Tampa bay Buccaneers owner Malcolm Glazer at Manchester United, have as much if not more say as the actual team manager and turn up as frequently on the sports pages as the players themselves. Emblematic of this valorisation of football as big business is the time given, via newspaper columns, to the vituperative opinions of the like of ex Chelsea chairman, Ken Bates, or the truly dreadful Alan Sugar, who retains a financial interest in Tottenham Hotspur after selling out to the Enic group of companies, but never is to be seen at a game.

G.K. Chesterton said that "if a thing is worth doing it is worth doing badly", and it is precisely such sensibilities that are extruded from the "game" of football, for it has all become "too serious" and consequently it is possible to argue that the "play" is no longer "play". Huizinga, ever the purist, wants to insist that as soon as there is a hint of professionalisation something of the "play spirit" is lost. Intriguingly the eminent French psycho-analyst Jean Laplanche argues in a similar vein with regard to psychoanalysis, "For me, psychoanalysis is not a profession. Once it tries to be recognised as such it loses its soul. Why is it not a profession? Because it cannot have a *Zielvorstellung*, otherwise known as a purposive idea." He gives the example of a child referred for analysis because of difficulties over going to school. He said that this always poses something of a difficulty because the parents and/or the authorities will wish that the child will come back as "a good student". But the analyst is likely to start by saying something along the lines of "all this is a joke, your parents want this, but we don't care, we will talk of other things, of whatever you want." He insists that psychoanalysis must put "all socially adaptive aims in brackets" and that is why it can never be a profession. Even though clearly people make a living from it.

This poses a problem for football. However much there may be a delight, an innocence, a faithfulness to this elusive notion of the "play spirit" in the disorganised "kick-about" somehow it is never the real thing. And as soon as there is a "proper game" it is automatically purposeful, the idea is to "get a result", which paradoxically does not necessarily mean that one has to be victorious. To touch on that idea of jouissance, so loved by French psychoanalysts, it is as if the sexual juice has been sucked out of the game if there is no meaning to who wins or loses. I shall always remember a Glasgow Rangers fan asserting in a faintly menacing fashion (a tad too close to my ear for comfort, prior to a pre-season fixture early one August, in Warmington House, the Spurs Supporters Club bar of that era), that "Rangers don't do friendlies!"

Football is concerned with particular value being given to virtuoso improvisation. Part of the aesthetic of its play is an unrelenting backdrop of high energy athleticism, in part somewhat brutal—the crunching tackle, the clash of heads—but all interspersed with those exquisite moments of what are affectionately referred to as "pure skill". Sacred geometry: the gracefully arcing cross à la Beckham being met by the perfectly timed header bulleting into the back of the net. Exquisite pleasure in seeing space, angle and weight of pass judged to perfection. Such inspiration, such improvisation is clearly linked or is more closely aligned to the artistic rather than the more prosaic, the purposeful or methodical so associated with the scientific. Adam Phillips writes of "the ordinary disarray of a psychoanalytic session", and this description is only too apt for any game. It can never go according to plan. Just as with the place of the analyst, the player can never know what to do in advance, as it were. Knowing what one is doing is as good as it gets, and of course so often it is only in retrospect that it is possible to glimpse any such knowledge at all.

Perhaps there can only be a value to football if it can enable our lives to become more fascinating, more exhilarating, more anguished, more agonising or whatever it is that can make our lives more alive. And possibly its particular virtue, if that is the right word, is that it allows us to accept aspects of ourselves and others that we might otherwise dismiss. Disavow is the psychoanalytic term. An instance of this would be the part that revenge and our lusting after it that is always already an aspect of much of our playing. A few seasons back Morientes, already faintly resentful to find himself out on loan from Real Madrid at the comparative backwaters of Monaco, had found significant gratification in playing a considerable part in seeing his actual paymasters dumped out of the Champions League. In the semi-final, playing against Chelsea, he was struggling to make much impact. His mood was barely improved by getting a painful elbow in the face from an irritable Desailly, all on the blind side of the referee. So imagine his release, that exquisite moment of ecstasy, when he finally broke free to rifle a shot into the roof of the net, giving Monaco the lead. But it was none other than the vengeful that drove him, following the exhilaration of that goal, mocking, taunting, tongue sticking out, towards the Chelsea Shed boys behind the goal. Something of this may raise the question as to whether what is taken to be a "good game" can be exempt from the ethical. An aside, but it is an almost immutable rule of thumb that any analyst who puts out a book with the word "ethics" in the title is invariably an incorrigible shitehawk.

For Huizinga our modern day sport has irretrievably lost touch with its sacred origins. Football has severed its links to the ethical. Previously great competitions in archaic cultures were always linked to sacred festivals, always indispensable in promoting health and happiness. Unequivocally football has become severed from these roots. It has become "profane", "unholy" in every way and has ceased to have any organic connection with the structures of our societies. So the grand and triumphal displays associated with the World Cup and its like, however important it may be for the players or spectators, all are consequently seen as ultimately "sterile . . . the old play factor has undergone almost complete atrophy." By no means daft he is only too well aware that such thinking will "run counter" to popular feeling. But nevertheless he insists that by an overemphasis on the seriousness of it all, something irreducible has been lost. Not to mention that to the consummate outsider it will all appear utterly ridiculous. In his faintly "boy scout", almost Winnicottian aesthetic, in order to genuinely play "a man must play like a child . . . if not the virtue has gone out of the game". It is as if only through the spontaneity of moments of grace during a game, through an innocence that is not self conscious, that it is possible to maintain something of these crucial "play" elements. Of course it is possible that any play can become so technically and tactically organised that the "genuine play spirit" is threatened with extinction. How often has one heard disquiet at a player's natural, more "instinctive" qualities being coached out of him (so exemplified by Steve Perryman's lament); of how the modern game has lost all sense of honour and "fair play"; how humour and ordinary decency inexorably is on the slide. Huizinga makes no bones about it. He is adamant. By implication football is "false play", it plays "false". Or to use his particular word "It's all gone *puerile* over there".

Well maybe. In spite of an acknowledgement of Huizinga's shamanic insistence of sticking to the high ground, I want to hold out for some other, more reckless reading of things. Perhaps more in accord with the old Spurs captain Danny Blanchflower's assertion that "It is football's power to so readily and regularly *corrupt* [my emphasis] emotions and senses that is the addictive and enduring appeal of the game." At one level it is incontestable: football has gone sour, bloated with greed and dangerously wanton with regard to its public. But such an emphasis risks missing the point. Whilst it is possible to be scornful of the insistence of football as madness, self elected madness in more or less manageable doses, let us allow that possibility to drift. One of R.D.Laing's colleagues Dr Hugh Crawford (with his years of ducking and diving through dwindling therapeutic house-holds) honed a particularly concentrated vision when it came to the damaged and the dispossessed. He thought that "care in the community" should mean a therapeutic household at the end of every street. (In the same way that pubs proliferate within our culture.) In many ways this is faithful to Foucault's conflicted reading of psychoanalysis where he ends up arguing against himself. Initially he saw psychoanalysis on the side of surveil-lance, incorrigibly linked to social control, but then he glimpsed a completely different vista of possibility. He came to see that it was only psychoanalysis that offered a sanctuary, a privileged enclosure where the mad might speak, and that it was ultimately on the side of the angels. And here comes football. All "care in the community".

It is as if Huizinga, unquestionably one of our foremost thinkers on play, loses his nerve. He gets off to a good start if we recall the association with that particular characteristic of play "absorption" and "the power to madden". In other words madness, something refracted through some other form of logic, possession and intoxication all come together in the mix. Allow that the word itself is problematic. Dr Roy Porter, the prolific and respected social historian in his *Madness: A Brief History* had this to say,

". . . madness cannot be defined. Aetiology remains specu-lative, pathogenesis largely obscure, classifications predominately symptomatic and hence arbitrary and possibly ephemeral and subject to fashion, and psychotherapies still only in their infancies and doctrinaire." It is not difficult to see that accusations of the sort that so bedevilled Laing's career, that lurking in what I am saying is a glamorisation of madness, are just round the corner.

Rather it is a plea to acknowledge that something that is in play, potentially in all play, genuine play, and certainly in football, is actually quite mad. Not as in psychosis and its attendant suffering but mad as beyond the rational, beyond meaning. Mad, mental, as in unalterably intense. The phrase "run riot" is what we all wish for our team. So that we can all "go wild". To recognise this is not to meekly submit to the puerile and the violent, but is more on the side of an embrace, an inclusion, a welcome even to those aspects of our being that lurk in the midst of playing football or that vicarious variation: watching others playing. Otherwise we are left with a vision of the "play spirit" which is too wholesome by half. All ugliness is to be airbrushed out. At one point Huizinga seeks to argue that if modern play was indeed genuine then we might anticipate that our civilisation would resume the "great archaic forms of recreation where ritual, style and dignity are in *perfect unison* [my emphasis]." This seems so saturated with a grotesque idealisation of the ancient world, with the overblown rhetoric of nostalgia for the imaginary, for the fictitious past. It is precisely this that psychoanalysis seeks so continuously to disrupt, prompting the letting go of a fictitious past. What football offers, amongst a whole host of co-existing possibilities, is a community where it provides regular and reliable opportunities for unadulterated heart thumping, adrenaline marinated, terrace Tourette's for the sane man. And an increasing number of women.

There is a delightful description by Harry Pearson in his book *The Far Corner* of one of the Ayresome Angels that bears such eloquent testimony to all this. "Peter attended matches splendidly decked out in a white umpire's coat with 'Boro' painted on the back and sleeves in red. He carried a red and white frying pan which a mate of his used to hit rhythmically with a red and white mallet. Once at a night game in Barnsley in the mid-sixties, Pete, immaculately coutured and brandishing his frying pan, had led a coach load of Boro fans in the direction of Oakwell. Turning left into a side street he'd found himself marching against a grim faced tide of West Yorkshire hard men. Emerging unscathed from his foray through this evil mare, he turned to see how the rest of the party was getting on. They weren't there. They'd turned right two streets before. Taking a deep breath, Pete plunged back amidst the Tykes, who, eyeing him with the same mixture of reverence and fear Navaho Indians reserve for *saintly and the insane* [my emphasis], parted and let him pass once more unscathed through their ranks."

Part of this madness is that there is an inversion of the more normative imperatives which seek to emphasise, to give the highest value to, a triumph over the irrational, the immature, and ultimately the sensual. For Freud it was those aforementioned women, as well as children, neurotics and so called "primitives" who are lodged within such a category of failure. It is as if this failure or refusal to let go of being under the spell of the sensual is to be damned, but (as Baudrillard would have it), that is all part of its charm. So often psychoanalysis rushes a little too quickly to place religion and sexuality under the sign of a "return to childhood", and yet there is something to that. Football may be similarly understood. As with children the pleasures that it affords are remarkably resistant when there is any call to relinquish them. Part of the irony is that Huizinga wants to handcuff play, genuine play, to the childlike, although no doubt he would want to differentiate that from the childish. But is it ever so simple? Football as community is rather like the child who is presented with the facts of life. However many sermonising admonishments emerge as to how it has lost its soul, its dignity, it just keeps on keeping on. Just as the child will insist, as one of my daughters did on being read for the umpteenth time the story of where babies come from, "Now, mummy, tell me the *real* story."

One instance of this was an incident up at Old Trafford in one of the innumerable meetings between Manchester United and Arsenal. In the last minute United are awarded a penalty, which had they scored would have won them the match. Van Nistelrooy muffs it, hitting the bar, and Arsenal—or at least some of their players—cannot contain themselves. Already angered by a collective sense of injustice, holding the United forward responsible for yet another Patrick Vieira sending off, we were subject to the unmitigated delight . . . well, we can leave the insufferably smug Manchester United fans to one side . . . of an up welling of overripe biliousness. It's a party. Particularly ignited by Martin Keown's impassioned contribution, the orang-utan impersonation not a millimetre away from Van Nistelrooy's crestfallen snout. More playground pushing and shoving, unleashing jeering and needling, all extravagantly explodes. Utterly puerile, utterly divine. But by Monday morning we were subject to the predictable plethora of hand wringing editorials all bemoaning the disfiguring of the great game reminiscent of the Reverend Thomas Vincent and his 1667 piece on *God's Terrible Voice in the City*, ". . . like the smoke of a great furnace, a smoke so great as darkened the sun at noon-day [it had been a morning kick off]: if at any time the sun peeped forth, it looked red with blood." A year later the Manchester United manager was still claiming that "it was the worst thing that he had ever seen in sport". Now of course he was referring to what takes place within the confines of any particular game, but nevertheless brushing up against the possibility of suppressing, just for a moment, all recall of the Munich air disaster so emphatically etched into the history of his club. In other words a dangerous loss of perspective.

As an impressionable teenager I found myself somewhat captivated by a deep throated, vein pulsating spectator standing just off to the right at Griffin Park, at an early autumn evening match between Brentford and Watford over forty years ago. "Come on you Bees, what we want is BLOOD!" Scorched in the memory bank, it distils the essence of that play spirit. It is not that there is no truth to the narratives of the tawdry and the trivial within the annals of football mania, of how the valorisation of players with "attitude" so often operates as permission to behave like a petulant adolescent. Nevertheless there is overwhelming evidence to suggest that there is something that there is little desire to submit to, as Freud and Huizinga—along with all those splenetic sports editors—would have it, that super-ego like call, that authoritarian insistence, reducible to the instruction "to grow up".

Not at all. And maybe all the better for it.

Trenchmouth

A wiry youth clutching a battered megaphone perches precariously on the sharp railings somewhat ominously fencing in the away support. They happen to be Paderborn's finest in the Ruhrstadium in Bochum. A blighted zone. Wiping his lank hair from his jangled eyes which only occasionally awkwardly swivel to look at what is going on out on the pitch, our man puts the megaphone to his lips and in best wailing banshee exhorts his "troops". They, in impeccable unison, eagerly respond by thrusting forth the fascist salute, screaming "Fuck Off" in perfect synchrony with the announcement over the tannoy of the Bochum starting eleven. In many cultures—Greece, Turkey and France all come to mind, this would be accompanied by the holding aloft of cascading flares, the unfurling of enormous flags and the incessant beat of the inevitable marching drum. One Friday evening in Bordeaux from behind the goal I saw nothing of the first five minutes of play, impatiently waiting for the smoke to clear. As the Porto fan sitting next to me in the Euro 2004 Semi-Final said, somewhat covetously, as we sat slightly glazed as a seemingly very ordinary Greek side stole their way to the Final, "Those Greeks, they turn their stadia into hell". To which a cursory glance at any Athens postcard rack will amply testify.

Another analogy that it is difficult to avoid whenever thoughts turn to football is a comparison with war. Something of the nature of the game encourages emotive terms, staccato phrases, the swelling thunder of the crowd, the back and forth, attack and defence, the in mixing of the graceful and the robust all lend themselves to notions of the war cry and the battle ground. Or as Desmond Morris would have it: all very tribal.

And this seems a place to begin. The thesis is that the origins of football are buried deep in our primeval past, when in order to survive we were driven (and this is Darwin) to evolve into hunters of meat. We had to get our teeth into something and this got its teeth into us. Initially the pursuit of wild animals was never a sport but immutably linked to this critical issue of survival. Quite simply it was a matter of life and death. So the original battle, war if you must, was between man and nature. Evolution-ary theorists will emphasise the gradual development of a whole host of attributes such as increased athleticism, heightened cunning, concentration, the development of strategies and tactics, and the perfection of the aim, all directed towards the ultimate goal: killing of prey. It is not difficult to glimpse that much of this operates as prototypical of playing football: the aim being "to kill off" the opposition, the last minute equaliser being "to come back from the dead", symbolically.

There appears to be a particularly English insistence of viewing football through the prism of war. Within any section of England supporters you are never far from those with an irrepressible urge to burst into song, with Second World War themes to the fore. "Ten German Bombers" and the "Dambusters" theme forever lurking to potentially stoke the fires of particular antagonism towards the 2006 World Cup hosts. Other countries who had previously been our allies are now frequently subject to renditions of "Where were you in World War Two?" and "If it wasn't for the English you'd be Kraut." Newspapers know that pandering to such sensibilities shifts copies. It was Piers Morgan, then the editor of the *Daily Mirror*, who was ultimately responsible for the front page "Achtung! Surrender" in the lead up to the Euro '96 semi-final. But he is far from alone in so wantonly stirring up racial and nationalistic tensions—and this is not just restricted to the tabloids, whose cameramen are ever hovering in the alleyways closest to the sites of potential combustion. But the English are not alone in making such connections: Diego Maradona repeatedly insisting that his "Hand of God" moment was amply justified by las Malvinas.

Possible origins of this repeated association can be traced back to the shift from hunting as an essential means of survival to hunting as recreation, hunting as a game. Desmond Morris is adamant: we make the transition from prey-killers to goal-scorers as an effect of farming. Of course this did not happen overnight. For nigh on a million years everything revolved around hunting and gathering, but gradually it dawned on people that it would be more cost effective to enclose and to domesticate our prey, and to sow and grow crops rather than wearisomely head off on another berry hunt. But the sensible and obviously appropriate agricultural revolution simultaneously left something to be desired, and that something seemed to be the madness of blood. Football, for the most part bloodless, now seen as merely a chapter in the history of blood sports. ("How come you support the Villa?" "Dunno mate, it's in the blood"; whilst Sven Goran Eriksson in musing about the superior ball skills of the Latin Americans suggests that "perhaps it is something in their blood"). The domestication of our world was accompanied by the imperative: get out of the house, experience the challenge and excitement of the chase, savour the ecstasy of the kill . . . and if the city dweller could hardly head off into the wilds, something of the wild could be brought to his front door. Ancient Rome, leading the way with regard to so much of what we take to be contemporary civilisation, via the construction of the Colosseum, the prototype of all modern football grounds, brought the delirium and the blood of the hunt into the heart of the city. As an aside, it is estimated that the capacity of the Colosseum was between 45,000 and 50,000, in other words roughly the equivalent size to present day senior football grounds. Grounds that are built to look like forts, like dug in encampments, mandalas of madness pivoted on a central axis: the force field, the park, the battleground.

And these prototypical stadia were up to their collective necks in blood (records show that in the first three months following the opening of the Colosseum approximately14,000 animals were slain), and as any who have been misled in attempting to track down the local football ground in Spain can testify, remaining vestiges of this legacy are sustained by the modern bullring. Coinciding with the unstaunchable shift of people from the field to the factory, a greater sensitivity to the suffering of animals seems to have led to the disappearance of that era of blood sports, ushering in the present day upsurge of ball games. Now it is not that there had not been some form of ball game in play, as it were, for some considerable time. Alexander the Great apparently enjoyed tossing some form of ball about, and the Greeks, later followed by the Romans, designed special "ball-courts". But somehow it was all rather downgraded, tame even, not the real thing, a bit like tapping a ball back and forth in a back garden; insufficiently challenging, too docile. Lacking the whiff of blood and madness. The poet Martial caught the mood of the moment with the line "The prancing pansy snatches at this ball . . ."

Yet there was a latency, and the latency was violent. Throughout the middle ages this mixing of blood sport, ball game and ritualised mayhem had been played out via vast sprawling, wild and uncontainable variations of folk football. Unequivocally "a man's game". Football had provided a form of unlicensed gang warfare, but this irrevocably altered in 1863. The TV series *Twelve*

Books that Changed The World, anchored by Melvyn Bragg (a Carlisle exile and Arsenal season ticket holder), flagged the importance of the first rule book of the Football Association. His claim is that this slim volume "totally changed the world. Before then football had been played in public schools and in the streets . . . great warfare that was banned for 200 years because it was so violent (not strictly true, although there had been repeated attempts to outlaw it, often on account of its association with political struggle and disorder) . . . so few people actually played football, just a bunch of public schoolboys. The rest of the country had a pig's bladder and used it as an *excuse to knock the hell out of each other* [my emphasis]." Bragg emphasised "the brilliance" of putting it in a set of rules, initially pasted up on the side of changing sheds for players to read out in order to familiarise themselves with it. It went round the world within about twenty years: British sailors, diplomats, and entrepreneurs exported it to places such as Brazil and Paraguay, Russia and China, and simultaneously foreigners came to England and took it back with them.

So whilst the validity of the thesis that football has foundational links with blood sports may be sustained, ("bloody football" as my wife might say) it is this immutable link with destructive, warlike urges that now come to the fore. Scoring a goal becomes a symbolic "kill". Football, now rule bound, becomes stylised battle. "La bonne guerre" as Robert Pires so eloquently calls it. Trophies no longer skulls on staves fondled as totemic power icons, but clusters of chrome phalluses gathering dust in gloomy cabinets. But crucially football historically has had considerable entanglement with political struggle, so frequently utilised to draw a crowd for quite specific political ends. A cause of enormously bitter popular resentment was the issue of enclosure: the eighteenth century development which led to the transformation of the face of so much of rural England, simultaneously ruinously displacing whole swathes of people

from land to which they claimed a variety of traditional entitlements. And what better way of organising some heavy duty
protest than announcing that a game of football would be played
on the enclosed land. In 1765 the *Northampton Mercury* advertised
a forthcoming match to be held on the enclosed fields. It is
intriguing to note that Northampton's present ground is called
Sixfields, for far more were at stake in what predictably followed.
Only too rapidly the football transformed into a political mob hell
bent on tearing down and setting fire to the hated enclosure
fences. Despite Northampton's finest dragoons arriving to stem
the flow they were helpless in the face of such a torrent of
resistance, and vast damage ensued. This is merely one example
of numerous instances where football operated as a pretext for
pitched battle in an attempt to find solutions to or at the very
least promote manifest protest as a reaction to social and political problems.

In a very real sense football has always sustained its place as
a terrain upon which certain class struggles have been played
out. Little changes as a story told by Pete O'Brien, my son-in-
law, bears out. In India on a business trip, a big game at the
weekend caught his eye. Casually suggesting to his hosts that
this is where he intended heading off to on the Sunday afternoon,
he was struck by a discernible resistance, anxiety even, that this
idea appeared to provoke. "Was it unsafe?", "Was it a sell out?"
were the understandable inquiries, yet somehow neither seemed
to quite distil the essence of the collective trepidation. Ultimately
persuaded by his unflappable determination, his hosts somewhat reluctantly organised a VIP enclosure (not what our Pete
had in mind at all . . . pay on the gate, buy on the street, what-
have-you . . . not that he was complaining). The crowd was
huge: 120,000 habitually turn out for Calcutta Cup Finals, and all
was utterly benign. The distinct impression was that the concern
had been marinated in class issues: football, irretrievably seen
as a lower-class or lower-caste recreation, was just not what a

respected English businessman was expected to have any truck with. As if some peculiar contamination might ensue, or as if Pete might witness some almost shameful aspect of Indian society. James Walvin's masterly account of the social history of British football *The People's Game* hammers home the unwavering link between football, that most common form of popular recreation throughout English history, and class struggle. Certainly since the fourteenth century the game, in some form or other, has been an incorrigible thorn in the side of the ruling classes, and their hostility to "the commoners" has been played out unwaveringly in relation to those who so enjoyed knocking a ball about "up the common".

But, as Walvin draws attention to, those ruling classes had troubles, hierarchical troubles of their own. As if there is something about authority—which may be another term for a relationship of dependency—that will inevitable provoke ambivalence at best, and outright hostility at worst. How many of us are aware that almost without exception all the senior public schools experienced major riots at the beginning of the eighteenth century. Both Winchester and Rugby had to call in the army (with fixed bayonets) in order to quell rebellious pupils. It looks as if Lindsay Anderson with his marvellous film *If* was something of an exception, someone who knew their history. Football, with its quality of anarchy, of disarray, was unequivocally implicated in all this, implicitly encouraging the young upstarts to overthrow their supposed superiors; recreational behaviour reflecting the hierarchical and violent microcosm of school life in general. Mayhem always lurking. A Frenchman, on observing a game in Derby in the early nineteenth century, posed an intriguing question "If this is what they call football, what do they call fighting?" Echoed nearly 200 years later by the small boy, barely initiated into the rites and rituals, blinking at the massed ranks of the Highbury east stand, plaintively asking of his father "Why is everybody so angry?"

And this is the uncomplicated basic thesis. Simplistic even. We cannot fail to acknowledge the warlike aspect of each and every football match: it is a battle. It is part of the attraction, the excitement of the occasion. By and large one or other side will have emerged triumphant, will have "got a result", which without qualifying adjectives you might assume means win, whereas habitually it has come to mean "getting something out of the game" by avoiding defeat. This final outcome, the issue of winning and losing, installs the symbolic element of battle. You really do not have to wait too long, almost as soon as the whistle signals the kick off the barely containable fury starts to unfurl: howls of "Gerrintahim . . . get stuck in . . . break his fucking leg" so commonly, so vociferously, and so urgently build momentum. I can still vividly recall the snarling features of our one-time manager, the fastidious toe-nail fetishist Alan Smith (who went on to higher things at Crystal Palace and Wycombe Wanderers), with his clenched fist perilously close to my nose as he prowled the touchline. "Up for it, Chrissy?" All in a last minute attempt to extinguish any desire on my part to "ponce on the ball", but rather to crank up the aggression, to drive me on to "annihilate" the opposition. To little avail.

Intriguingly quite what this arousal of such violent, antagonistic emotion is being used for sets up competing and conflicting narratives. A prevailing view is that there is something mildly therapeutic going on. That through an involvement in either playing or watching a sport such as football we are enabled to express and thereby dissipate these aggressive and destructive urges. The Gestalt therapy motif: we will all feel better for beating the shit out of that cushion. But will we? This is the overworked "safety valve theory". By hurling oneself into the fray, either through immersion in the tensions of actually playing, or by submitting to the contagions of screaming and cursing so characteristic of the football crowd, we "let off steam", we "get it out of the system". The idea being that it is inconceivable that we would not feel some form of frustration, some form of pent up rage; it just goes with the territory: the territory of being human. There will be inevitable conflict, call it ambivalence, in all relationships as all relationships are characterised by the threat of loss, of abandonment. And if it is not possible for that anger, that hate, to be expressed or at least straightforwardly acknowledged, it will so often be directed towards ourselves. This is an aspect of the elementary Freudian thesis in *Mourning and Melancholia*. So via an unleashing of this potentially congealed anger, congealed or even unconsciously turned on ourselves to defend against damaging our love . . . we sustain it as uncontaminated by ambivalence, at least consciously . . . we are at the site of an enormous and valuable release. And we are all the better for it. Or at least that is the idea.

But the competing thesis is that football, far from assuaging such aggressive feelings, only serves to aggravate them. We are all potentially aggressive, principally as a defensive reaction to a perceived threat either to ourselves or to anyone or anything that we give value to. And football above all else insistently provokes a threat: the threat of losing, and so whilst this threat exists aggressivity will only be intensified. For some of us that is all part of the buzz, the routine home win over lacklustre opposition somehow leaving one strangely flat, deprived of the adrenaline rush. So long as there is some genuine struggle going on, sufficient tension will be maintained and that crucial ingredient of uncertainty holds sway. Relief—the dissipation of that tension—will only come with the final whistle. But whilst there may be some evaporation of our aggressive urges on those occasions that "we", our side, have come out on top—the anger burned off, all subsumed under an excited triumphalism, yet wasn't it all rather trumped up in the first place? All only inaugurated by the football itself. In other words it was a massive displacement. There may very well be the enjoyment of the glow of victory, indeed that may take us away from other concerns

—but these will still exist, merely deferred, merely postponed. Symptom removal is what psychoanalysts would call it. And it is frowned upon, although there are some of us who, were we able to guarantee the removal of a symptom would only too eagerly bottle it, stick our name on it, and presumably make our fortune.

Then of course there is the small matter of those for whom there is no release, no triumphal surge: the losers. The aggression, the tension has hardly found resolution, far less dissolution. In many cases all is accompanied by an intensification of frustration and overbearing peevishness. Hopefully contained and ultimately short lived, but as ugly scenes in the tunnel after the recent World Cup play off between Turkey and Switzerland exemplify (a Swiss substitute was hospitalised after a frenzied attack by a cluster of Turkish players and stewards, Turkey having lost on "away goals") the claim that football invariably operates as a "safety valve" appears deeply contestable. Nevertheless there is an incessant volatility to our aggression. It is only too easy to engage in some form of displacement. We endlessly shift our angers and frustrations, so often enmeshed with those pathetic concerns over power and prestige, and it would hardly be surprising that football provides an avenue for some out-let. But equally it can work both ways: frustration and despair over the performance of one's team can be taken out at home or at work, as cats and performance levels in major industries know only too well. But football and aggression are incorrigibly entangled, and there is a simple gratification in getting out in the fresh air and having a good bellow that in all probability does nobody any harm.

But it would be simplistic to leave things at that. The idea that football has hitched itself to our fundamental warring impulses is difficult to shake off despite an initial resistance. It is not uncommon for "midfield generals" such as Patrick Vieira or Roy Keane to be described as "a good man to have alongside you in the trenches", inevitably provoking the response "What fucking trenches?" After all the term "handbags" is so commonplace in describing a typical flare-up in so many a game, so the vocabulary of war just does not feel quite appropriate when thoughts turn to genuine slaughter. But such considerations are quickly swept aside as we are caught up in the fervour of being "On the march with Kevin's army" ("Kevin" being dispensable, but never the military motif). Football unequivocally is linked to considerable aggression, violence even, but is it genuinely a substitute for war? Perhaps we ignore the place that war has in our subliminal ideals at our peril, for the issues of glory (and what did Danny Blanchflower call football?) and its counterpart: shame, cannot be overestimated. We might note a curious paradox: if we were to ask people would we have the history of war expunged from our history, all substituted by a narrative of peaceful transition, were such a thing possible, we would meet considerable ambivalence. For all the blood, the battles, the heroic efforts of our ancestors, the memories, the legends, are all crucially linked to a communal ideal. And it is difficult to shake off. Difficult? Well nigh impossible.

Yet ask the same people would you want to start another war today and hardly any would show much eagerness for such a proposition. For it is only when forced upon one, when the other's injustices leave no alternative, that war is now found permissible. Yet there is something of the pugnacity, the lust for the afore-mentioned glory, even an ambivalent fascination with the horror that appears to have been passed down from our ancestors. To quote William James, "War is the strong life." An extreme life, life on the edge. All with this emphasis on strength. Somehow there seems to be an insatiable demand for power and domin-ance that is as old as the hills. Despite all the wailing, the envy, the denunciation of the Abramovich millions and the effect on the Premiership (the clamour, the chorus line of disapproval, the prophesies of "ruination") the ancient Greeks knew the score:

"The powerful exact what they can, and the weak grant what they must." For no doubt all other clubs would be only too likely to behave in highly similar ways to the fashionably despised Chelsea.

Somehow our ancestors have bred pugnacity into the bone and marrow of our being, and there is little evidence of it disappearing. For it is not as if the bestial and horrific aspects of war are in any way hidden, and culturally the drive for looting and plunder is never far from the surface. "Shag your women and drink your beer" is the plodding and unhappy chant of so many "troops" as they peel out of the railway station. Although officially it is invariably projected onto the other: here in England we have a "defence force", the armed forces, ostensibly solely existing in the cause of "peace". There is something almost schizophrenic in our attitude: on the one hand we note an international rationality whereby it seems as if surely it will be possible to ultimately find our way to agreement in each and every conflict, only for this to be read as wishful thinking. As a utopian ideal. As a fantasy. All in flight from the implicit recognition of the immensely destructive aspects of all wars. But on the other hand we can decipher a set of assumptions that are crucially characteristic of war. The first is the issue of patriotism. The idea of supporting a particular side is for the most part upheld as a virtue. Neutrality, the "objective view", is almost always ruled out or at least thought of as distinctly odd. This is framed by the idea of war as "the romance of history". War principally as a narrative of good triumphing over evil. If it had never existed we would have had to invent it, as it works as it continuously retrieves life from a form of degeneration, an incipient flatness. War romantics can promote it as human nature at its "highest dynamic", without which there would be no scorn, no hardness, and no valour any more. "Fie upon such a cattle yard of a planet" might well have been a Victorian rallying call. Cue William James, for such sentiments might well appear to belong to some other era. But have they genuinely disappeared?

There is something of this valorisation of strength, of hardness, and of daring, all entangled in an emphasis on superiority, even of a moral high ground, all redolent of the war apologists, that suffuses the inevitable imaginings that accompany a World Cup. Whilst the "minnows" invariably claim to be happy merely to "be there", collecting the loot to plough back into grass roots football back home (or line the pockets of their Football Association), surely England cannot be alone in being subject to the curious pandemic of World Cup hype. Without exception it builds up a head of steam every four years, with muttered polemic increasingly debating the merits of Peter Crouch's ability "on the deck", the proliferation of serious thoughts about "placing a few bob on England", and the emergence of an epidemic of flags fluttering off car aerials and upstairs windows, reaching a crescendo about three weeks before the tournament begins. "After all, you never know . . ." All to end in crushing disappointment, only partially offset by a month of afternoon drinking and a curious eagerness to get back for the big one: Togo v Poland. For somewhere in this is the idea that—as in war, so in football—some essence of our nationality is at stake. A manifest display of ability in either one or the other operates as a marker of the nation's health (but more people swarmed into Copenhagen's main square to celebrate returning from Sweden in 1992 as European Champions than were there on Liberation Day in 1945).

War, and now its substitute football, takes its place as an ideal whereby a judgement of the qualities and virtues of a nation are weighed in the balance. As if an essential element of any nation in which the people can come together to employ all their powers collectively (as Uri Geller gets his spoons out) is facilitated by these two potentialities. Other sports don't quite do it, however gripping a recent Ashes series might have been, indeed generating the headline "Cricket is the new football!" Something of this was captured by a conversation overheard on the British Rail local service limping into White Hart Lane twenty-four hours after England had won the Rugby World Cup. One man was discussing the previous day's rugby. He was saying that he had not particularly noticed that much furore, that much excitement after England had won in the last minute. His friend, who acknowledged that he hadn't been "arsed" to watch it, made the hugely pertinent comment, "If that had been us, beating Germany in the World Cup Final with a last minute penalty, the whole country . . . we would still be off our heads dancing in the streets." For some, a frightening prospect.

It is as if victory is unconsciously felt to be the marker of the totality of all virtues, the corollary being that defeat is an effect of some vice or feebleness, and luck is ultimately cancelled or cultured out. Fidelity (team spirit), cohesiveness, tenacity, the heroic, intelligence and inventiveness, all saturated in high energy and vigour all converge into the winning ethic. And this is true of football every bit as much as war, which drives these elements so much to the fore. As if no ordeal is comparable, as all else is degenerate, all culminating in enervating depression. So much of this is linked to a basic assumption that our origins are embedded in pain and fear. The psychoanalyst Otto Rank's seminal book was called *The Trauma of Birth*, peddling the idea that for all who made it through, pain and fear along the birth canal is everybody's lot. As a consequence of these beginnings there is an unacknowledged assumption that any transition to an age of peace and a straightforward pleasure economy will unavoidably lead to degeneracy and decline. In other words we fear an emancipation from fear. We are driven to inculcate it with whatever means are at our disposal, and a weakened, a weekend diluted form, are those frenzied anxieties that so grip a nation on the eve of a crucial game.

Whether it be a military life or that of a football club certain characteristics prevail.

For some they designate a particular charm, for others (and Stan "Sixty-a-day" Bowles comes to mind) incorrigible oppression. Discipline, an atmosphere of devotion, of service, of co-operation all directed towards the common goal of ultimate triumph so much the order of the day. In both instances an emphasis on force, the "gerrintathem" imperative. And whilst no-one can seriously deny the cost—human, financial, and ethical—that war involves, this can never be the full story. Unconsciously war, with its emphasis on the thrilling and the tragic, is felt to be worth all this because it is an antidote to anxieties with regard to cowardice, weakness, and passivity that lap at the margins of our being. We cannot afford to live in a peace-economy. And football, with all the attendant acknowledgment of the paltry and the puerile, stands in that place with the ever present fear of loss. There is an immense importance of fear in our lives. No uncertainty, no risk element, and all would degenerate. Fear operates as a particular intelligence, and where can we find it? In a secular age we can no longer assume a fear of God. In a basically peaceful age, post Cold War, there is no longer the fear of the enemy (although some would have it that, in this age of terrorism, we are already in the "Third World" war): in our materialistic world, at least from a Eurocentric view, there may be found the odd residues of fear of poverty if we become idle, but the fundamental fear that few escape from (Tantric hermits on Himalayan hillsides notwithstanding) is the fear of inferiority. And this leads back to the hooligan mythology, and the parade ground mentality of the assistant manager: an unequivocal emphasis on toughness. The war ethic praises a certain callousness, a hardness, all now read off as something of merit. It is now what is necessary, and thereby dignified, for a common cause. Competitive passions, contempt for softness, a whole seriality of the so called "manly" virtues ironised by the adversities of an away day to Grimsby, start to proliferate.

Some take this very concretely. Stan Ternant, one time Burnley, Bury and Gillingham manager amidst a host of other football involvements, was renowned for carting his players off to "boot camps". These players would be exposed to quasi life threatening situations, paddling across fjords after a twelve mile hike chased by dog patrols, for example, precisely to set them up to deal with fear. To do their maximum under stress. To make them communicate better. To make them honest. The theory being that under pressure they learn about themselves, and Stan could also learn about them. Watch somebody in a highly stressful situation and you will know how he will react in a game later in the season. That was the policy, and the claim was that you could see the same look in the footballer's faces as they prepared to leave the dressing room as could be seen in the eyes of soldiers as they go into battle. The stresses are enormous: they are fighting for a renewed contract, fighting to show each other what they can do, and they can go from success to fiasco in a single second. The consequences are not the same, that's all. You were left with the very real sense that if Ternant did not see that focused, cancelled stare, that player was not long for his dressing room.

But it is intriguing to recall that there have been times when football, and a continued interest in playing it, was recorded as singularly "unpatriotic"—utterly divergent from any war ethic. This was most certainly true during the First World War, despite there being that legendary game played in no man's land against enemy troops. Many refused to forgive the football community for seeming to carry on regardless after the outbreak of war, and this antipathy was reflected in poor attendances once peacetime football was resumed in 1919. Initially everybody praised the magnificent contribution of rugby players who had selflessly joined up and headed off to the killing fields of northern France, whilst professional football unpatriotically kept on keeping on.

Or at least that is how it was portrayed, so much an effect of class divisions, increasingly reflecting the disenchantment those "public school/officer class" gentlemen had with football. People were even starting to bet on it (disgraceful!), and there was an intensification of professionalisation, leading these so called gentlemen to turn towards the seemingly less tarnished game of rugby.

By the Second World War political and nationalistic considerations were emphatically refracted through football. Not difficult to proceed yet again along the lines of "Blame it on the Germans" but actually they hardly had a monopoly on such considerations. Whilst it is valid to suggest that fascist regimes were always quick to utilise their sportsmen and women as substantiating claims of racial superiority, footballing patriotism was hardly new. Within the British Isles there had been the annual antagonisms of the England-Scotland clashes. Clash being the operative word. Spite and malice so often being the order of the day as the Scots repeatedly sought to establish some instance of superiority over political masters. But with the advent of the World Cup, initially played in Uruguay and won by the host nation, it was possible to witness ideological as well as national tensions on full stream. Both the 1934 and 1938 World Cups were won by Italy. The teams were rigorously overseen by the fascist government who, like their German counterparts, was desperate to bring honour to their visions through football. All utilised to buttress a particular regime and ideology.

But this time around in Britain there was a far greater interweave between the war effort and the football authorities: football facilities, in the shape of inner city stadia, and players, quickly taking up their place as PT instructors in the recruitment camps, were immediately placed at the disposal of the War Office. Initially organised football was suspended, but following discussions with the Home Office it was decided to rapidly sort out a revised schedule of fixtures. Despite warnings of mass gatherings the one sporting event that Winston Churchill appeared at was a football match, acknowledging the value that he placed on it. Eager to keep public morale on the up, a vista of a winter without any football was too bleak, too excruciating, to contemplate. The government implicitly recognised the *therapeutic* value that football had for a country. Less consciously acknowledged was the therapeutic value war provides. George Bataille recognised that Nietzsche had seen that the rigours of asceticism and holiness had lost their attraction in a contemporary world, that only revolution and war were able to provide comparably exhilarating experiences. That without hesitation war has become the counterpart in modern societies of the "paroxysms of the festival". War, the time of excess, of violence, of outrage, is analogous to the festival in that it gives rise to "monstrous and formless explosions that serve to break up the monotony of normal existence." Bataille was clear. This is a shocking interpretation, "but it would not do to close our eyes. To do so would be to fail to understand the sacred, as it would be to fail to understand war." As it would be to fail to understand football.

Sanity cannot propose a simple pleasure seeking economy. It leaves too much out. Something else is left to be desired. It appears that there is an insatiable desire for something more malign, for the essentially agonising and antagonistic quality of struggle that plays such a crucial part in our enjoyment. And so much of this is underpinned by fear, which is not to suggest that this is the only stimulus for arousing the higher, the more excessive echelons of our enjoyment. Simultaneously tucked into this are the dubious claims of the eternal verities: that any implicit or explicit exhortation to savour those martial virtues are of an absolute and fundamental value. And what "all" believe in will grip the individual. For now we are all "on the march" with "whoever's" army, some indeed purposefully heading in the direction of the aptly named "Pride Park" up at Derby County.

For there is pride in the collective, and our own individual pride rises in proportion. We may recognise a fundamental human need to belong, but merely to belong to a community, a particular neighbourhood, with the street parties, the neighbourhood watch meetings, and the summer fêtes can start to feel anti-heroic. Anti-erotic even. No honour there. But to sign up for the terrible football team, to lock onto that particular madness, that way glory beckons.

The Tableau Vivant

For the vast majority of us the principle involvement in football will be through watching others playing, either in grounds or through the keyhole of television. Inevitably almost everyone will have had at least some rudimentary experience of playing, but for the most part it is football as spectacle, as something that we are engaged in looking at, that holds sway.

We watch people watching. We don't see what they are feeling, but we may only too easily hear what they are saying, and it is what they are saying that may give us some clue as to what they are thinking, but are not as yet aware of . . . in other words are unconscious of. The knowledge that doesn't know itself, as the French psychoanalyst Jacques Lacan used to say. And of course it is what we are unconscious of that is so crucial to the psychoanalytic project. What we see, what we take in and are taken in by, are these terraced, these serried rows upon rows of animated, discordant, attentive faces. For the most part this is blurred, blurred because people are constantly on the move, and are moved, because above all else football seduces, leads astray, moves, grabs us.

78

Or not as the case may be. In the 1970s I was involved as the "house therapist" in one of the Philadelphia Association's community houses in the East End of London—in Dalston to be exact. The Philadelphia Association was a psychoanalytic organisation set up by, amongst others, the somewhat controversial psychiatrist and psychoanalyst R.D. (Ronnie) Laing. A sort of Brian Clough of psychoanalysis, if you will, never less than interesting but perhaps something of a bully. Both men living under the sign of hero and troublemaker. One of the things that I involved myself in was the quasi avuncular activity of introducing some of the people who lived in the house to some local cultural activities, the "Alternative Technology Festival" out on Rainham Marshes, for example. Inevitably (how could it not suggest itself) one Saturday a trip to my beloved White Hart Lane was proposed. Despite promises of being able to watch "the greatest goalkeeper of his generation", the legendary Pat Jennings, not to mention being able to witness some of the finest "hooligans" in the land at close quarters, one member of our party was singularly unimpressed. In truth, that may have also been so for some of the others. Either too polite or too transferentially cowed to draw much attention to it possibly, but for this young German man the whole thing was a ghastly mistake. Retrospectively it was fascinating to see seduction work in an opposite direction. For many of us there can be an intense desperation to get into the game. A desperation perhaps only matched by the need to piss, to shit. There may be an attendant anxiety that our precious match ticket will somehow be snatched away from us, mysteriously or magically jump out of our pockets, so there is impatience not only to get to the ground but an insistent restlessness until we are "safely" inside. But for our German man it was "inside" that made him feel quite the opposite: a sense of considerable disquiet. He said that what struck him was the irretrievable ugliness of the whole situation: the unrelenting concrete, the metal crush barriers (there still being terraces at

Tottenham at that time), the being buffeted around by the crowd and ultimately the aggression, both out on the pitch and baying forth from the spectators. It was not so much that he was frightened but rather, from an aesthetic point of view, he was appalled . . . and wanted out of there. But twenty minutes into the game this was no simple task, and a short while later I saw him sitting with his back to the game, disconsolately muttering that it was "like being in a fucking prison". At half time I found a sympathetic turnstile operator and his suffering was over. Not to mention mine. But of course he had a point. Beauty is in the eye of the beholder. And for Lacan the emphasis on or the idealisation of beauty, and all those claims for "the beautiful game", are invariably that which veils a fundamental horror.

The urge to be the same, to conform yet simultaneously maintain some modicum of difference appears to be at the heart of the human condition; it is probably innate and most certainly inescapable, this human attraction to rivalry. It is the counterpoint to that fundamental aspect of our being: imitation. The narcissism of small difference is what it is called. Rivalry is a fact, it is by nature biological, and consequently so is human disorder. Football is an outlet for these perfectly ordinary tendencies that can manifestly get out of hand—if not always then at least some of the time on the edge of disorder, both amongst the spectators and those out on the park. But something appears to bind the whole occasion, to structure it, this business of watching others watching others playing, and that something can be called possession. It might even be that I find myself absorbed in watching another watching precisely in order to remove, to distance myself from this. Possession so often being associated with madness, and watching football has that quality, that extraordinarily seductive moment or moments in which we are subject to that irresistible invitation, that call of contagion pouring down from the terraces, that "Lets all go fucking mental". Or to put a more pompous resonance to it all, following the Russian cultural theorist Bakhtin, we could call it "the carnivalesque". Heroic because it is so flawed.

Ian Ridley, the erstwhile *Observer* football writer who "fulfilled a dream when he became chairman of Weymouth, his home town club" had this to say of his first game in that role, "As the fifth goal went in (they went down 5–0 to Crawley Town) it dawned on me that I could no longer behave as a fan (aka one possessed). I could not berate the goalkeeper or the defence, could not scream at the manager. I was chairman of the club and certain standards of behaviour were expected, not least by me." The fan, the fanaticism, "the demonic possession" as a theologian might refer to it, "hysteria" if you happen to be a psychologist or psychiatrist, the "trance" or state of "ecstasy" if an anthropologist, all now had to be suppressed, but of course that did not prevent Ridley from describing an 8–0 drubbing of local rivals Dorchester Town on Boxing Day six months later as "a glorious high". Drug wisdom and craziness, all in manageable doses doled out at 3 o'clock at the insanity factory, otherwise known as the local stadium, and we have not even begun to talk about the absurd if not completely cuckoo sums of money invested in all this malarkey. As I think that Ridley found to his cost.

Whilst it is clear, indeed how could it be otherwise, that the modern overblown and highly commercialised professional game as we know it today bears little resemblance to what James Walvin in his admirable social history of British football, *The People's Game*, calls "the *wild* mediaeval football". The curious thing is how often it was football that continuously cropped up in government prohibitions, and clearly those prohibitions were a response to something—and that something continues to suffuse the situation to this day. Many of the strengths and insanities that inform contemporary football bear a considerable similarity to those found in pre-industrial football, for in some form or other football has been a fact of English social history since the beginning of the fourteenth century, if not earlier.

William Fitz Stephens, Thomas à Becket's biographer, wrote of an early instance of something very analogous to football taking place in London somewhere around 1180. But listen to this: in his description of those who came "to view the contests and in their fashion sport with the young men . . . there seems to be aroused in these elders a *stirring of natural heat.*" Heat and its link to the sexual, the passionate, and the hot bloodied. It is possible by a meticulous trawling through legal records from the thirteenth to the nineteenth centuries to trace out an unwavering narrative of football having a constant association with violence and social unrest. This is Walvin, "It was, in brief, a game which at times came perilously close to testing to the limits the social control of local and national governments." Perhaps difficult to sustain a thesis that this is entirely true to this day; after all, no politician appears sufficiently unselfseeking to attempt to ban it, something that was repeatedly attempted throughout the 1300s. Football was so frequently perceived as "interfering with more useful pursuits . . . particularly archery." Yet one got the sense that Thatcher would have given it a go if, for a moment, she had thought that she could have got away with it. But this does not go away. In November 2005 there was a certain amount of concern as England were due to play Argentina in a so called "friendly" in Geneva only 100 miles down the road from a World Cup play off involving Switzerland and Turkey. The convergence of fans posing a "security problem". Mutterings of calling the England game off from Head Office.

But back to earlier times, it is almost impossible not to recognise the madness that lurks in the heart of the beast. So often the game was an ill-defined contest between indeterminate clusters of young men, invariably played in riotous and raucous fashion in tightly restricted inner city streets. Usually giving rise to unconstrained uproar and potential for damage to property, not to mention the opposition and inevitably attracting to the fray anyone with an appetite for havoc and general disarray. Then it was the players rather than the spectators who were held responsible, there being little or no distinction: everyone just piled in. Characterised by these qualities of uncontainable surges of energy and chaotic exuberance football appeared to pose endless problems for the maintenance of law and order. Here is a description of a "game" in 1772 in Hitchin, now a fairly unremarkable small town hovering in the radius of resentment that rings London, "The ball for a time was drowned in Priory Pond, then forced along Angel Street, across the Market Place into "The Artichoke" beer-house, and finally goaled in the porch of St Mary's Church." It is precisely this anarchic force field that sweeps all before it, all subservient to the manic drive striving to sustain some other vision of what it is to feel alive—all so exquisitely captured in the marvellously random mayhem of the beer advert where a ball appears to "innocently" drop from a window ledge to inaugurate the "kicking off" of a mass street-game.

So what about what is actually said, for psychoanalysis is always concerned with the specificity of the actual words used, the particular vocabulary of the person coming for analysis? Perhaps it is beyond the scope of this survey to distil the multiplicity of terms with regard to football that go to make up the private language that will always inform the ways any distinct community will speak of and with itself. There will always be jargon. As with psychoanalysis, so with football. For a sustained and erudite study of the game's particular language you could do a lot worse than Peter Seddon's *Football Talk*, or even better is Leigh and Woodhouse's *Football Lexicon.*

But let us note that there are a number of problems whenever it comes to *writing* about football. It is manifestly clear that such writing, entirely like writing about psychoanalysis, is hugely varied in both purpose and quality. Although a dying form, the running story of the Saturday afternoon match for the local evening "classified edition", so that those who watched the game can relive most of its kicks in biased recollection, can so often serve as an excruciating form of folk narrative. Similarly some of the tangled case histories appearing in the plethora of professional psychotherapy journals, so that those who were not present for that particular therapy can relive, kick by kick as it were, various prior assumptions via biased recollection, can hardly be sustained as "literature". Excruciating or not "the classified" formed an integral part of so many a Saturday evening in the British post-war era. London used to have three different papers, and the scenes described in Ward and Alister's *Barnsley—A Study in Football 1953–59* "were repeated across the nation . . . the Barnsley streets became a sea of Green Uns as fanatics read the Sheffield Star reports. They met their wives, and depending on their mood after the match, took a night on the town, perhaps a meal at the bus station café and a visit to one of the eight cinemas or a dance hall. Occasionally a man could be seen reading the Green Un behind his partner's back as they waltzed."

Football rarely provides the material for sustained thoughtful-ness if only because the actual activity of playing is inherently simple. Fifty years or so ago we had then Tottenham manager Arthur Rowe's mantra of "Keep it simple, keep it quick" and nothing has fundamentally changed. The football enthusiast, unlike his cricketing counterpart, is not exactly bombarded with excellent books on the subject, despite, more recently, some notable exceptions. We always had those "Chelsea Casuals": Brian Glanville, Hugh McIlvanney, and John Moynihan, and before them John Arlott (who although known principally for his cricket commentaries wrote beautifully about football), the exquisite Percy M. Young, the sublime Arthur Hopcraft and almost donnish Geoffrey Green. But post-Hornby, or perhaps more accurately since Eamonn Dunphy and his Millwall book, the list starts to lengthen: Davies, Hill, Kuper, Pearson and Schindler to cite just a few. Also looking further afield there is David Winner's exhilarating *Brilliant Orange: The Neurotic Genius of Dutch Football*, Phil Ball's *Morbo: The Story of Spanish Football*, not to mention the delights of Franklin Foer's *How Soccer Explains the World*. So it is spreading, but nevertheless football is notoriously a sport without much of a literature despite Albert Camus once writing that "All that I know most surely about morality and the obligations of man, I owe to football". He had turned out in goal for Algeria "B" but unfortunately he was never to develop this theme.

Equally the players and managers often appear to be unable to speak without resort to clichés, otherwise known as truths exhausted through repetition, or mumbled inarticulacy, principally an effect of the incorrigible difficulty of putting into language the intricacies of a virtuoso performance or the hapless inadequacies of the bungling player. This is the philosopher A. J. Ayer, a long term Tottenham addict, in a piece written for the *New Statesman* in the early 1960s, "White missed an easy chance in the opening minutes: just before half time Jones had what seemed a good goal disallowed for offside: Allen and Dyson missed open goals . . . Smith scored with a shot which the goalkeeper had no chance to save." Habitually so elegant when defending the merits of logical positivism, when called upon to describe what took place during a game he is reduced to a level of the most mundane of football writers. The difficulty being that there are not many of us who can find great eloquence when either speaking or writing about states of passion and possession. The truth is that every discourse on football (and this one is no exception) can only and always fail—miss its object as it were—precisely because it makes an object of it. Any such musings can only circulate around the phenomenon, always tearing at the leash, so eager to enter the maelstrom, to cast off, to let go, to stop writing *about* it. To get out on the park. Or into the stadium. To taste the delirium.

As another philosopher, the phenomenologist, Maurice Merleau-Ponty, a regular at Lacan's bridge evenings, said

"If you want to know about swimming, jump in the water." But somebody who knows something about the delirium of following a sport is Johnny Green, Gillingham supporter, one time manager of The Clash, and author of the marvellous *Push Yourself Just A Little Bit More*. This is his story of following the Tour de France, but he might just as well have been writing about the World Cup, the Copa America or the African Nations Cup, even the closer-to-home European Championships. He evokes the era of Neal Cassidy, saying of Jack Kerouac that "he knew and loved those fizzin', poppin', burstin' fireworks . . . he'd have dug the miles, the movin' on, the adrenaline rush . . ." And that is just the high of chasing a game. Once you are there (this is Green again) "You're yelling and screaming before you can think, before you can organise a coherent word. Just roaring from the depth of your being. Consumed." He is writing about cycling, but it was honed on the terraces of Priestfield. After all is not his club's history called, *Home of the Shouting Men*?

But what of the fans, the "people" who are after all the vast majority of those who go to make up the so called "football family", the familiars of the "beautiful game"? Something that is endlessly repeated is an emphasis on banter. On the terraces, in the stands. It is what players miss: the dressing room banter. It is what the anthropologist Desmond Morris in his book *The Soccer Tribe* described as "a capacity for rapid verbal riposte". He sought to link this with a mirroring of, in other words an identification with, the deft movements on the field of play. The humour that is deployed is so often saturated with the trickery and feints of the ball player. As if the aim is to leave the other stranded, trailing in one's wake, just as with the opponent out on the pitch. Inevitably such moments are highly context specific, and to quote them is to lose their sting. But you might get the gist of it from odd cullings of graffiti: daubed on an inner city wall were the words "Leeds United are magic", and someone had chalked beneath "Watch them disappear into the Nationwide".

Schadenfreude, the exquisite but malicious delight in someone else's misfortune, suffuses the situation. It is not so much that you want someone to win, but you *really* want someone to lose. In Britain whole pubs across the nation explode into delirious delight when in the spring of 2004 Porto's last minute goal knocks a hole through Manchester United's season and dumps them out of the Champions League. And there is not a Porto fan in the place. The psychoanalyst Winnicott, who can sometimes feel almost shy, certainly coy (not that this inhibited him from opening a bottle of wine when his 6pm appointment came round) was adamant. Murder is part of our being. An illustration of this would be the idea that our leaving the parental home is "symbolic murder", something is killed off. Something that once existed: our childhood, no longer exists, is dead. Game over. The New York analyst Michael Eigen writes in his book *Ecstasy* that "We are always killing each other off as part of the back drop of unconscious fantasy . . . the urge to kill is part of every interaction".

Excessive maybe, for is that really the backdrop when, for example, I thank my postman for delivering my mail? But something of that must be in play when it comes to football whether it is exemplified by exhortations to "kill off the other side", "put the nails in" or when the "injury time" (curious phrase?) equaliser is described as "coming back from the dead". Clearly murderous is not all that we are, but we are not without it. Destructiveness is part of aliveness, and we need to feel alive to our destructiveness in order to feel genuinely alive. And for some of us the serious business has got to be live. This is Johnny Green again, "I need a buzz. I need live. I love to be behind the goal . . . to see the ball coming at the net. Players' faces and shouts. Not just the man with the ball. To take in all the pitch, everything. I love to be part of a football crowd . . . in the crowd feelings let rip. Passion is shared. I can let loose the caged beast within me."

So much of this is magnified within a group. It has to be said that groups or crowds do not get a good press from psychoanalysis, so much of it based on the work of the French crowd psychologist, Gustave Le Bon, who wrote in 1895 that "The age that we are about to enter will in truth be the ERA OF CROWDS." But as far as football is concerned it is the "era of hooligans", those words "football" and "hooligan" having become so indelibly entwined.

By and large psychoanalysis bought the story that, principally as an effect of imitation, behaviour in a crowd would invariably sink to the lowest common denominator. Crowds suggest and are eminently suggestible. The moment of the gathering into a crowd will create a collective into which the individual will be submerged, all swept up by unconscious processes. And unconscious processes are linked to the more primitive or, following the claims of a progress narrative, earlier stages of our development. Crowds regress. And it is contagious. "Isolated he may be a cultivated individual; in a crowd, he is a barbarian" or as Jung said "Man as a particle in the mass is psychically abnormal". In other words will go a little crazy. The basic theory is that in a very large group the collective psyche will be more like the psyche of an animal (leaving aside the question as to whether animals have "psyches") and this is the reason why the ethical attitude of any large organisation is inherently dubious. The presence of so many people together exerts tremendous suggestive force. Any individual in a crowd so easily becomes the victim of his or her own suggestibility. Again Jung, "The group because of its unconsciousness has no freedom of choice and so psychic activity runs on in it like an uncontrollable Law of Nature. There is thus set going a chain reaction that comes to stop only in catastrophe". As if he could see into the future and the future was Heysel—the Heysel stadium in Brussels being the venue for the 1985 European Cup Final where thirty-eight Juventus fans lost their lives following crowd trouble.

If football is akin to a religion it is a debased, discredited, indeed pathological religion. Such assumptions presumably would be the orthodoxy. But we must hold on to the recollection that so much of this theorising about crowds was set in the context of the peculiar positioning of the State: in fascist Italy, in communist Russia, and above all in Nazi Germany. The State having moved into the place of God, whilst simultaneously omitting or ignoring that fundamental axiom of mass psychology whereby the individual will always become morally and spiritually inferior in any large group. Or at least that is the claim.

From about 1970 until the mid-1980s the phenomenon known as "the English disease" took hold. Whilst it is clear that this was far from a great era in terms of the national side—England having gone into inexorable decline after Bonnetti's flapping in Leon, and dismally failing to qualify for the next two World Cups, it was a completely different story at club level. Although the somewhat reviled Don Revie and his Leeds side broke up without really fulfilling their full potential, Clough's Nottingham Forest won the European Cup twice and Liverpool were, well, LIVERPOOL! Utterly dominant both at home and abroad, they remorselessly accumulated domestic and European trophies. Launched into this golden era of ascendancy by Bill Shankly, Bob Paisley magnificently grabbed the baton and reeled off the accumulation of twenty Cups and championships between 1974 and 1983. Yet this was a period that only the most myopic could fail to acknowledge was disfigured by the ugly and highly contagious proliferation of "it all going off". Those hooligans. And it had an export licence. Curiously for someone who spent a considerable period of time in and around football stadia there are merely two or three incidents—all abroad—that are the only vivid recollections that I have of the phenomenon. Perhaps an effect of always playing on a Saturday afternoon rather than being in a stadium, but it wasn't that I was not watching football. Not at all. Perhaps I was just not watching. Just dissociated.

The first was at the 1974 UEFA Cup Final when, after a few days of acid haze in Amsterdam, I had arrived at the Feyenoord ground in Rotterdam on a pleasantly sunny evening. But by half time it had all turned sour and the Tottenham manager, the much revered Bill Nicholson, was obliged to get hold of a microphone and to go behind the goal in order to make desperate attempts to quell the mini riot. He articulated what so many of us have felt on too many occasions: "You make me ashamed to be an Englishman". In his biography *Glory, Glory. My Life With Spurs* he spoke bitterly of how angry he had felt ". . . that English fans had tried to smash up part of our opponents' fine stadium . . . the perpetrators are not lovers of football. They see the game as an excuse to provoke trouble and start fights . . . pillaging and looting and causing mayhem". In his anger he was not alone. The mild mannered middle aged Feyenoord fan sitting next to me suddenly whipped off his finely polished brogues, and armed with one in each hand, was ready to take on all comers, only to be dissuaded by the realisation that what was provoking his ire was actually some two hundred or so inaccessible yards away.

Next up was six years later in Turin and England are playing Belgium in their first game in the European Championships. Seemingly a reaction to the mediocrity of the English performance fights started to break out behind one goal, and the Italian carabinieri, never known for impeccable cool, managed to gouge a sizeable hole in the Stadio Comunale's electronic score board with an wayward tear gas canister.

Twenty years later it is water cannons in Charleroi. Brian Glanville in his *Football Memories* writes despairingly of the problems in Marseilles during the 1998 World Cup, "Thank God, I did not have to cover England, with its 'minority' hordes of brutal, brutalised fans ravaging Marseilles . . . here they were again, an alienated underclass that could express itself only through violence. A miserably untalented subspecies . . . why should other countries be subject to the barbarian invasion?"

What he articulates is in so many ways incontestable. And having witnessed at first hand him freely and affably mixing with the "barbarian hordes" on numerous England away trips, often in preference to hobnobbing with the somewhat cliquey press boys, any charge of snobbish disdain must be pushed aside. Despite his memorable analysis of the phenomenon as "the revenge of the D-stream". And it is serious. He mentions the "poor gendarme . . . all but killed [by] a sinister, organised group of German neo-Fascists in Lens [at the same World Cup] . . . no real explanation, unless you classed it as a resurgence of that dreadful German nihilism that characterised the Nazi years". And there was the aforementioned Heysel, the stadium in Brussels where thirty-eight Juventus fans were crushed to death, many under a collapsing wall, after fighting broke out in the unsegregated Z block at the European Cup Final of May 1985. I had gone there with one of my most long-standing football friends, Nick Harling. Having procured tickets off an amiable tout we had headed off into the surrounding area to find some food, only entering the ground about five minutes before the appointed kick-off time. That time came and went, and much to our bewilderment everybody stood around by their seats seemingly equally puzzled. It was only gradually that word percolated through that the game had been delayed because of crowd trouble, but at that time there was no sense that anyone had died. Over to our right behind the goal a large section of terracing was strangely more or less empty, abandoned. As it included a section where we were to meet one of our friends after the game, and as nothing else was happening, we decided to head off round there to see what was what. On our way we encountered little knots of ill tempered Liverpool fans belligerently howling for the game to begin, clearly unaware of what had happened. There was no difficulty in gaining access to the somewhat ramshackle terrace behind the goal, where we picked our path past numerous scattered and forlorn clusters of abandoned shoes and clothing, to join assorted somewhat dazed looking fans to slowly piece together the story of the harrowing events. Even then the numbers that had died were understandably vague. The atmosphere was one of slowly building numbness, and to this day I have no idea whether it was appropriate to play the game—it all felt utterly irrelevant.

Four years after the events in France I was standing outside the stadium in Busan before South Korea's opening game in the 2002 World Cup. I am trying to sort out tickets for my wife and myself, only to be somewhat disconcerted on hearing that the going rate is about $400. It so happens that a delightfully obliging local student sorts something out about half an hour before the kick off—at face-value. Whilst all this is going on I am talking to a football friend, Danny Murphy. It could be said that Danny's life revolves around football, which is not to say that is all that holds his interest. But much of the time he works until he has accumulated sufficient funds to support the next trip, the Tiger Cup in Indonesia or a World Cup qualifier in the Solomon Islands, that sort of thing. Suffice to say when it comes to these matters, Danny has been round the block a few times, and it is no great surprise to find him in Busan checking out the ticket prices and keeping an eye open for the bootleg drinking tents that are supposed to line the riverbanks in the less salubrious parts of town.

Meanwhile it looks as if the entire city has dressed for the occasion in a red "Fighting Korea" top, and at least half have indulged in face paint. At other grounds it has been noticeable that "fans" had been bussed in from the local communities to dress up and "support" one of the foreign sides. "Fans" who could not have told you the name of one—not one—let us say, of the Bulgarian side that they purported to support. Yet all is happy, benign even, with a fair smattering of the host nation's opponents, the Poles (genuine Poles) in peaceful evidence. Yet Danny is contemptuous. "You know Chris, it's not that I'm condoning what went off in Marseilles, but this lot . . . it's all gone Disney. Give me the other lot any day of the week."

I remember this occasion so distinctly, in part as an effect of the delight at gaining entry, but more importantly because in part I shared Danny's sentiments. But it is a conflicted call. Freud was virulent in his advice "to distrust our antipathies", and yet it is hard not to share some antagonism towards the unrelenting ugliness that can cut its swathe through Europe. But at the same time is there no antipathy towards a disproportionate fascination with it all, the valorisation of its camaraderie, its violence, the blood and honour? Those books, that film *The Football Factory*. Its sociology has been raked over, done to death and is not about to be reprised here. Some may claim that concealed beneath the baggy trousers of academic rhetoric is a considerable hard-on, drooling over further fetishised details of the violence. But for sure, even those of us who had no desire to know anything about hooliganism probably know all they need to by now. Psychoanalysis might stray into some analysis of the phenomenon in an attempt to gain some kind of grip on its historic persistence and returns. Or it could box clever and play on a reversal, to see the "hooligan" in psychoanalysis, Freud's imperious barnstorming through the Twentieth Century. As the French analyst J-B. Pontalis said in his *Love of Beginnings* it all goes grotesque when psychoanalysis "gatecrashes everywhere, when it affirms that it is the interpretation of all possible interpretations." When it all goes bully-boy, when you are not saying what you think you are saying, you are what *I* say, what psychoanalysis says.

But what I want to explore is the part that hooliganism plays in our imagination. Possibly there is an inevitable blindness, a wilfulness that besets us, whenever we seek to understand or enter into dialogue with some other world. But to call hooliganism "other" is already to beg the question. Or to put it another way, when we seek to confront or to contest a system of thinking or set of values, to castigate a particular way of being in the world, what may happen to our own? The psychoanalytic claim is that it may very well tell us more about ourselves than we care to acknowledge. Freud in *Totem and Taboo* wrote of the myth of the primal horde. That original band of brothers, all rivals in pursuit of mother, who unite in the murder of the father. Who via the ritual re-enactment of this murder in the form of the sacrificial meal enact some form of deferred obedience to the Law. Kinship will always imply participation in a common matter or substance, and in this instance the shared substance is blood. We just don't seem to be able to extricate ourselves from the red stuff. Perhaps what is difficult to accept is the ineradicable violence at the heart of the social tie—the Glanville position (but why pick on him for we are all implicated), it is a group phenomenon, the implicitly liberal position, involves the desire to shed, to dissociate from *our* shared discourse of shame; from the blood on *our* hands. To lodge with the folk devils, the "hoolies", all those aspects of our own violence in the history of our culture. The gaze of the innocent observer is always already ruled out, for this is the impossibly neutral gaze of the one who falsely exempts themselves from our concrete historical existence.

For when it comes to the psychology of the group our collective identity is always violent. We come together, we unite through placing the enemy outside, but the violence is always our own. At the very least we all share in the history of colonial land theft: a violent history indeed. In part this is faithful to the ideas of Le Bon whose claim in his 1894 *Psychological Laws of the Evolution of Peoples* was that it was "the dead [who] govern the immense domain of the unconscious . . . It is by its dead that a people is led." In other words his "unconscious" is a hereditary, but crucially a racist, colonising unconscious.

Those terms "D stream", "subspecies" with the link to the ill educated, the thick, the bonehead primitive, returns us to that area of Freud's thought where there is a complicated linking or the establishment of an equation between childhood and the primitive. And psychoanalysis plays on the rim of undecidability when it comes to childhood. Is the child always less than? Or is there something of considerable value that we can glimpse, gain access to, by a realisation of what we have had to repress. Or suppress, and have to continue to do so—possibly at great cost—by our compliance with the imperative to let go of childish things. Can we ever entirely let go of a fascination with the psychic life of the child? Do we have a greater respect for the child? Is there something more fulfilling in the immediacy of their being? Or more crucially do we really advance, as the progress story lays claim, from child to adult, from primitive to civilised? From the hallucinatory wish fulfilments of infancy to the potentially megalomaniacal, ultimately paranoid desire to bend the world to our will, to pathetically lord it over our little empires? All strutting like politicians. What else are those colonising, appropriative, imperious advances of the West? And what of the sado-masochistic nuances that inform the psychoanalytic tie?

But there is a difficulty with this, for it is hardly sustainable that the darker, more aggressive, rivalrous aspects of human nature are continually suppressed. Rather what is overwhelmed to the point of extrusion by precisely such emphasis is quite another story. The history of the more collaborative and cooperative elements in our make-up. Possibly as a counter to the somewhat "essentialist" views of a rapacious mankind we should note contemporary historiographical initiatives which propose a more complex pattern. Early humanity's spread and advance is understood less in terms of violent conquest but more in terms of community. The traditional ideas of "invasion" and "conquest" whether it be the Romans, Anglo-Saxons or Vikings are now subject to revision, allowing for the possibility of arrival by invitation. And let us never forget that UEFA, FIFA or whoever, are never slow in coming forward when it comes to raking in the ticket cash. We are "invited to apply ..."

The Independent columnist James Lawton describes an incident that is so familiar, so worn out through repetition. He was sitting in a dockside café in Cagliari during the 1990 World Cup. Visitors and locals were enjoying their coffee, their newspapers, the exquisite sunshine, or just idly gazing at the big ferry boat coming in from Genoa. Then the English arrive. Yelling, throwing about their collective weight and their beer cans, abusing anyone who stood in their marauding way. In a couple of minutes the terrace was bare of all but the invaders. "Civilisation has simply retreated." My emphasis, Lawton's words. And sixteen years on anyone who was around the centre of the old town in Nuremberg on the day of England's match with Trinidad would have had to have been seriously dissociated not to have discerned something similar.

But perhaps on closer examination whilst it is true that we "grow up", that hopefully we have every desire to contain our violent impulses, is there not an increasing shakiness with regard to this "civilisation"? It all starts to look increasingly precarious if we accept that our inherited burden is to bear the repressed history of our ancestors. Football commentators are fond of the phrase "it's a big ask", and they do not come much bigger to ask of the "civilised, liberal minded" to carry the weight of what is most emetic, most offensive and ultimately destructive about the hooligan. In part this is faithful to Freud. He recognised modern man's legacy as one of bearing those repressed histories of an earlier, so called more "primitive" world. Perhaps equally primitive will be those times that we can all be swayed by participation mystique. When we will all be caught up in what those images of hooliganism so often suggest: a theatrical staging. All subject to the gaze of the CCTV camera, the performing of a tableau vivant, posing for Sky News. And Lawton en-roles, performs the role of the one, the nostalgic one, who upholds the "true" values of what England stands and fought for, "to recall a time when they arrived in Europe not to make a scabrous, shaming nuisance of themselves, but to offer their lives in the cause of freedom." Maybe there is no exit, no one can escape from merely signing up for an allotted place in the unfolding drama, certainly not me.

The exemplary economic strategy of modern capitalism is outsourcing: subcontracting another company to do the dirty work of material production. Ecological and health regulations are far more lax in Indonesia, let us say, than in Germany, so let us outsource production processes there, thereby projecting, disowning responsibility for any of the "necessary" violations. Meanwhile in America in February 2003 we find the Department of Defence in the shape of Donald Rumsfeld and his taxonomy of the terrorist threat musing over the relationship between the known and the unknown. Manifestly we have "the known knowns", that which we know that we know: we abhor hooliganism and its boorishness, the "them". With this comes "the known unknowns", in that we know that there are some things we do not know: how to eradicate it. After the hiatus in Japan in 2002 (possibly an effect of travel costs and the "feminisation" of the policing, albeit with a Samurai presence forever lurking) to say that it is a thing of the past is to risk complacency—but to claim that it is as prevalent as ever is alarmist. It ebbs, it flows, it dies down, it is displaced. But as with those Samurai, it forever lurks. After all for the most part Germany and the World Cup was a blazing, convivial success. But then there are "the unknown unknowns": all the things that we don't know that we don't know. Otherwise known as irretrievable ignorance, habitually projected into the mass of those anonymous members of the "D-stream", all "thick as shite". But what psychoanalysis has an unflagging interest in is Rumsfeld's crucial fourth term: the "unknown knowns". These are things that we don't know or don't want to know that we know. In other words the Freudian unconscious. And it is this knowledge, a knowledge of not merely our violent colonising history, but the disavowed beliefs, suppositions, corruptions and grotesque practices such as the institutional initiation rites, the misogynistic office life, the alcohol saturated weekends (need I go on) that we pretend not to know about; don't want to know about. Seek to ignore, despite their place as the obscene underside of popular British culture. Rather let us bask in the spurious comfort zone of an unceasing but increasingly worn out dualism: us and them. All so redolent of our relation to the insane: place them outside the city gates, lock them in the insanity factories, the day centres, place them in "bins". For after all these folk devils are rubbish, white trash, animals, a "subspecies", are they not? But as Danny said "It's not that I condone . . ."

It has to be possible to disapprove of hooliganism without suppressing the recognition that it raises unsettling questions about none other than ourselves. Of course there is a danger in any exuberance, in a triumphalism that may spill out into an orgy of destructiveness. Innocent people can get hurt. Nevertheless there is a danger in rendering a particular culture synthetic, all anaesthetised by the trappings of a free T-shirt and some face paint. On rare occasions it is even the player who will complain at the library-like atmosphere in the stadium. For example Roy Keane and his "prawn sandwich" rant: the Manchester United player complaining that so many of the spectators at Old Trafford were more interested in the quality of the wine served in the executive boxes than what was taking place out on the pitch. So much of football is now played principally for television audiences and the easy pliable tastes of the multitude. And spectators are implicitly encouraged to become part of the spectacle: to dress up like donkeys or giant carrots to clown in front of the cameras, all to take their place in so called "non-stop entertainment" so encouraged by emotionally incontinent producers and milked by over indulgent commentators.

Just for a moment allow the thinking of the novelist J.G. Ballard to lap at the margins of these considerations. His theory is that the psychology of the business park and the shopping mall operate at a systemic level to bring about a deadening of human sensibility. Seemingly nostalgic for Cold War dualisms, associated with a clarification of the real conflicts between certain aspects of the human psyche, he rails against the dangers of the consumerisation of our world. "Consumer capitalism has a voracious appetite, it needs to keep us buying." Cue the utterly emetic Peter Kenyon, speaking of Chelsea's empire building plans, "The first objective is to own London. When we talk about internationalising the brand, the first thing to do is get critical mass within our own territory." Certainly he succeeds in generating massive criticism and loathing of his club.

Meanwhile the grand narratives of political ideologies have fallen away, despite Ballard's claim that vast Darwinian struggles unfold between competing psychopathies, the competing psychopathies of capitalism, fascism and communism. His concern is with this anaesthetisation that inexorably spreads via the homogenisation and sanitisation of our being. Where Bentalls in Kingston-on-Thames becomes the equivalent to a modern day hell. "You see these huge galleries with people wandering around, and it's a world where the most important human decision is what sort of trainers you are going to buy". The "suburbanisation of the soul" is how he describes it. The enervating qualities of all this evoke Kubrick and the "Clockwork Orange" effect, violence being the remedy rather than the symptom. But of course we are in danger of an excruciating romanticisation of the hooligan as they now take up their place as foot soldiers in a glorious crusade to restore vigour to a jaded universe. Any idea that what is at stake—even at the most subliminal level—is a disruptive strike in the direction of Acacia Avenue can only appear somewhat fanciful. Particularly as soon as some historical perspective is brought into play, for there is considerable evidence to suggest parallels between the Circus Factions, the rival groups of charioteer supporters from the first centuries A.D, and the more recent Soul Crew and Inter City firms. Or the acknowledgment that the so called "hooligan" is only too likely to be first in line for the latest special offer from those Bentalls shelves.

Freud sought to derive the origins of our ethical life from the ambivalences of mourning. Via identification it is possible to respect, grieve even for our enemies. This is a form of honouring the dead, those that we have killed off (which is perhaps what we would like to do to the hooligan) without things becoming unbearably pious. He saw ambivalence as being right at the heart of our emotional life. This is not to say that such conflictual feelings can be resolved or surpassed. "Nothing is resolved, everything is lived through" and maybe ambivalence with regard to the hooligan phenomenon is as good as it gets. To merely engage in a hand-wringing denigration comes on as just too easy, but to engage in the sociology of justification leaves too much to one side. However, we are left with the feeling that the whole terrain has been "done to death" and that there is something of this murder, this killing off, this rendering invisible that the hooligan seeks to redress.

This question of visibility, of identity, is exacerbated by various degrees of capitalisation on our enslavement. Replica shirt anyone? For some this colonising involves the passive submission to the infantilisation of our world. We become engulfed, we acquiesce through inhabiting a totally controlled and manipulated environment. How many more times are we going to be told that such and such a game is "the most important" in so and so's history. It is as if we are all shackled to our expensive seats, compulsively compelled to watch the shadowy performance of what is falsely taken to be reality. Note that Monday morning ritual of the man arriving at the office after his team has lost, the "Don't even mention it!" all suffused in glazed despair. One might assume that, at the very least, there had been a death in the family. We submit compliantly to the reduction of our sensory and sensual experiences to a potentially minimalistic digital seriality of 1–0, 2–1 and so on into the abyss of the penalty shoot out. This simulated reality becomes a stand in for what we might take as "real reality". At some level it begins to look as if we are lost. Entangled in a nightmare. Football as commodity, but a degraded, anaesthetising commodity that consumes us as we consume it.

For as Ballard says, we cannot stop buying, we are eaten up by such imperatives. The content may differ, but structurally all remains the same. As in Plato's cave, all is semblance, all is propped up by the gnawing belief that outside the world that we actually inhabit, the potentially shallow world of football, of fashion, of "all tomorrow's parties", there is a "true" reality. Despite all being simultaneously seduced into the spectral show of Serie "A", La Liga or the overblown Premiership. Or whatever it is that turns us on. And of course this operates for psychoanalysis: transference, the love tie between patient and analyst, is not the "real" thing. That is always elsewhere, only for that to be virulently refuted by yet another outraged "patient".

The followers of the psychoanalyst Jacques Lacan are fond of the term the "big Other", a virtual symbolic or social order; a network that structures reality for us, that pulls the strings. For despite what we might think, we do not say what we want. "It" speaks for us, we are spoken for. And so often football can seem so very like this. Our diaries are organised around "the fixtures". As in the love tie, he or she is unbiddable, he or she is "Arsenal". And the curious thing is that if we do not submit to be spoken for in some way ("what, you don't support anybody!?") it is as if we can be in danger of being consigned to the place of the irretrievable alien. So "other" as to be invisible. Unsupportable even. As with the Rolling Stones imperative that "he can't be a man if he doesn't smoke the same cigarette as me", football operates as an enclosed universe. Yet it is an elite form that is open to all, as psychoanalysis should be, and here lies a crucial element in football's ongoing capacity to fascinate. Some uphold the day in May 1979 of the Dandelion Market gig by the band U2 as having particular significance. They played a free outdoor concert for a largely teenage audience who had been unable to get in when they had played at the neighbouring McGonagles club in Dublin the night before, emblematic of their founding attitude towards inclusion and exclusion with regard to their world: the world of rock 'n' roll. It is where football and pop and rock collide, and psychoanalysis is in there too, for all are informed by the drive to give a voice and a face to the forgotten and the dispossessed. All are welcome until they have to lock the gates. Well maybe not at Old Trafford or much of the Premiership ("The greed is good League" as Brian Glanville has called it), but if football is your drug it really is not too difficult to cop off.

But that belonging may be at a considerable cost, and I am not just talking about the price of tickets. For entangled in all of this is this issue of the visible, our visibility. Fear of the loss of our precious individuality, of becoming merged into the mass, may lead us to endeavour to stick out, to hit out. And so much of this will be framed by a peculiar fantasy. Psychoanalysis, or at least the Lacanian version, wants to subvert the more obvious or common sense notion of the spectacle. It wants to disrupt the more habitual subject-object relationship. Rather than looking at things in terms of the spectator looking, staring transfixed at the reality of the match, all informed by a set of prior emotional predispositions, we are asked to change focus. This is now centred on the point from which the viewed object, in this instance, the match, gazes back. More formally put the gaze is not so much on our side of things but on the side of the "object", the game itself. Curiously it is the blind spot in the visual field, it is purely phantasmic, but it has effects. A good example of this would be the "haunted house": as we stumble up the hill it feels as if it is looking at us. Not gazing but staring.

How can "football" be looking at us whilst we are looking at it? In one sense this is impossible to see however hard we peer. However it can so often feel as if we are all being watched. The fundamental fantasy is neither with regard to the actual game itself nor all the imaginings that may surround it, but that of the imaginary, inexistent gaze observing us all. The gaze from above, from within, from the very heart of it all, from wherever, framing everyone with the idea that someone out there is looking at us. But as the Beat author William Burroughs said "the paranoid always has some idea of what is going on", all now subject to the unrelenting swivel of the CCTV camera. Put another way, we are the objects in someone else's dream, the dream of the "big Other". This serves as the ultimate guarantee of our being. A reversal of the contemporary nightmare of always being subject to unwavering panoptic surveillance, now it as if we only exist in as far as we are looked at—all the time. The hooligan is merely one of the many who have bought into the fantasy, both embracing it and seeking to strike out against its somewhat oppressive qualities. Note those households and the Chinese take-away shops where the television set is invariably on, yet nobody is watching, the flickering set merely serving as that minimum guarantee of the social link. As I head off to Portugal the parting shot, the compulsive, irresistible flourish is "Look out for me on the telly". A little, harmless trace of the madness.

Living the Dream

The sense of time in football is so clearly that of dream space for principally it concerns itself with the present, the immediacy of the what next, the anticipated, the about to be. Just as when we dream. Except for all those sepia tinted occasions of nostalgic wallowing—which is not to say that wallowing doesn't have its hugely enjoyable place. And the past has a price: Sotheby's sold a Tottenham v Sheffield United 1901 FA Cup Final programme for £14,400 in the early months of 2003. An expensive compensation for never having played in a Cup Final oneself.

So it is not that there is no past worth mentioning—that is of course absurd—but so often it is in an attempt to place some nuance on the unfolding and unrelenting present. Any attempts to formulate a future (such as West Ham need to find seven more wins to stay up, or every side bottom of the Premiership at Christmas goes down—these are the sort of calculations that I am thinking of) will always founder. Always occluded by the persistence of the dream, they will always collapse under the urgency of the "what next?" That which is right before our eyes, inaugurated on each occasion that the referee blows the whistle to start the game, so linked to the "taking each game as it comes" mantra. Note that commentators invariably use the "instantaneous present" ("Beckham passes to Owen . . .") despite describing something that has always already happened, albeit so recently as almost to be in the present. Yet the description is never in the past tense, and this will be picked up and imitated by countless children and park footballers. Barry Davies in the early 70s on Bruce Rioch "You can't give a player with that much class that much time" being a particular personal favourite on the odd occasion that I rifled in a goal. The past is not so much a completed stretch of time but that which survives into the present. Indeed the past can only seep into the present for it is only possible in dream space to dwell in the now, the eternal present. Memory, or archived memory, as in records logged in the Rothmans, can not so much be lost, but reinterpreted, mythologized. The past either recedes into insignificance (for example Chelsea never beating Arsenal in the Premiership used to be an insistent incantation) for that which existed in the past, now erased as unimportant, has ceased to operate. Or is furiously clung to as a form of protective cloak. The future is in part unimaginable, loss unbearable, so all sorts of magical possibilities drift in and out of consciousness. The dreaming never stops, for however many times reality, the numbness of defeat intrudes, the dreaming knows nothing other than to re-emerge.

Quite literally we dream of football results, usually forever discarding the occasions when our dreaming has no bearing on the actual result. Only once can I recall correctly forecasting a score in a dream, and it goes a little way towards refuting Freud's insistence that our dreams are wish fulfilments. It makes no sense to me that I would dream of Tottenham losing at home in a fairly meaningless end of season fixture against Aston Villa. I had deserted the cause, heading up to Scotland, and had, as far as I was aware, utterly forgotten, suppressed even, the previous night's dream fragment. It was now about 4.45pm and I was shuffling out of Livingston's ground when the results started to drift out over the tannoy. And then, there it was: Tottenham had gone down—nothing so inherently surprising in that—but it was the score: we had lost 4–2, at home. It was that which pricked me into recalling, suddenly, that was precisely what I had dreamt the night before. That score, one has to admit, is or was barely predictable, and my hunch is that such occurrences are far from rare amongst football supporters.

Indeed my brother tells a story of an intricate dream concerning his team's match, involving the fluctuating scoreline, roughly the timing of the winning goal, and the name of one of the goalscorers (George Best as it happens). As he sat down to watch "Match of the Day", not knowing the results, he mentioned to a friend the details of the dream, and lo and behold, the game unfolded in precisely the way that his dream had predicted.

One of my "patients" tells me a story of his son correctly predicting the *exact* attendance figures at Highbury minutes before they were flashed up on their electronic scoreboard. And again from my brother an even stranger tale of the uncanny: a mate of his had returned from Wales a few days before Liverpool were due to meet AC Milan in the Champions League Final in Istanbul. He came bearing gifts in the shape of a Liverpool v Manchester United programme from a game at the back end of the 1980s which had ended in a draw. A 3–3 draw. For some time during the season in question my brother, a Manchester United follower, could not escape an insistent foreboding that Liverpool were going to end up as "Champions of Europe", and his friend's gift had prompted a thought. Armed with the magic programme he headed up to a bar to watch the game with a number of his football friends, announcing in no uncertain terms that the score would be 3–3, and that Liverpool would go on to win on pens. Less ostentatiously he had handed over the programme to a particularly avid Liverpool follower. At half time he implored disconsolate Liverpool supporters not to leave, as they would miss an incomparable moment in the club's history, although even he was becoming a little half- hearted in this assertion. We all now know what happened, and next day the Liverpool fan couldn't contain his understandably compulsive desire to tell all about the "magic programme".

Could it be that such instances are testimony to the idea that football, on occasions, can provide access to altered states of consciousness leading to strange and stranger forms of knowledge? Which is not to suggest that I have any coherent explanation as to how I, or anyone else for that matter, could know *in advance* what a particular score might be. Of course it would be absurd to propose that only football can offer us such access. After all psychoanalysis can too, for both are entangled principally with the complexities of trance and possession, of telepathy and of ritualised fusional states.

Curiously psychoanalysis in the sense that it is a "clinical" experience that concerns a particular person operates in a similar way to the random disarray of a game of football. Quite simply one can say that no person, no subject can ever be a repetition of another: a psychoanalytic situation is always singular. Just as a game of football is; it is never the same, is never repeatable. All part of the allure. Those who have established some other form of dream space will in all probability never come to understand why anyone in their right mind would drag themselves out on a miserable night in February to watch what will inevitably be two not particularly successful or attractive sides. If it was a night at the theatre the play would have closed long ago. And yet people go in their thousands. For it is never the same, even if it is at times, unbearably repetitive. And all of this—football, dream and so much of psychoanalysis are informed by rapture. Simply look at the eyes in the photographs of both players and spectators. A sort of zen state, a particular form of attentiveness. Freud called it "free floating", yet simultaneously utterly focused. Almost like the hippy chorus line of "Be here now". Trance now on the side of the analyst. On the side of the spectator, and curiously enough, on the side of the player too.

So many are enmeshed, so many to their detriment. An emphatic symbol of precisely the nightmarish quality when Premiership dreaming congeals was the large-scale hoarding up at the Leppings Lane end of Sheffield Wednesday's ground, Hillsborough, in October 2004: NEXT HOME GAME vs. HARTLEPOOL UNITED. A marker of an excruciating decline. And they never saw it coming. Like so many others who were "living the dream" (as Leeds United's failed impresario Peter Ridsdale just down the road so poignantly put it)—they were utterly enraptured when the likes of Paolo di Canio and Benito Carbone pulled on the famous Wednesday shirt. And why not? They were far from alone. The list of those who have slipped from the top flight (flights of fancy?) reads like a litany of dashed dreams: Nottingham Forest, Wimbledon, Derby, and the aforementioned Leeds, to name but a few.

As has previously been mentioned more often than not it is women who will point it out, possibly because they are a little less subject to it. About an hour before the kick off, roughly a mile's radius from the stadium, it is possible to witness that peculiar phenomenon of men entranced. Of men mesmerised. It is something to do with the purposefulness of the walk. On those thankfully rare occasions when one is approaching a ground when the match has been called off the difference in the quality of the stride between those who are now drifting disconsolately away and those still hurrying towards the assumed kick off is palpable. Psychoanalysis, dubbed by some as being "merely a chapter in the history of trance states" frequently seeks to suppress its associations with hypnosis and mesmerism. It proposes another identity, almost as if these associations will forever handcuff it to the shaman, the trickster, the snake oil salesman. Freud was sometimes too concerned with propriety and that has left its legacy. But both psychoanalysis and football bear the hallmarks of precisely these phenomena.

The art of shamanic trance-facilitation utilises repetitive verbal signal patterns and rhythms, often delivered through the chanted word, sometimes backed up by the beat of the drum. For many years the French national side, "Les Bleus", were always accompanied by their jazz band; the Spaniards by Manolo, the Valencia café owner who will always haul out his big drum; and now we have the fairly excruciatingly leaden "Sun band" at all of England's games. But for the genuinely surreal head for the small mining town of La Louviere, just south of Brussels, who play in the Belgian first division. Situated on the half way line opposite the main stand you will invariably find a small brass band. But what is so odd are those moments when they will, with wild abandon, suddenly blast away with no seeming connection to anything that is happening on the field of play—a haphazard and exuberant sort of madness. It is contagious. It inexorably spreads.

A question that will always elude the most meticulous analysis concerns the inauguration of a new football song or chant. Many are anthems that are lodged in a deep historical tradition, such as West Ham's "I'm forever blowing bubbles", possibly ingrained via the particular aptitude of the plaintive wail of "Fortune's always hiding, I've looked everywhere". Not too many trophies to be found in the Upton Park cabinet. Other songs appear as a tribute to a particular player: West Ham providing us with their rendition of "Paolo di Canio/ Paolo di Canio/ Paolo di Canio/ Paolo di Canio" done to the tune of "La Donna e Mobile", the volume of which is inevitably turned up by the opposition's fans chiming in with "Paolo di Canio/fuck off to Lazio".

But it was David Thomas, an *Independent* journalist, who drew attention to the strange and spontaneous up-welling of a new Bobby Zamora song, seemingly out of thin air. Down on the South Coast with Brighton, Zamora had been rattling in the goals (76 in 125 games, highly impressive), and was understandably a fan's favourite, and they came up with "When the ball hits the net/Like a fucking rocket/That's Zamora" sung as a variation of the "That's Amore" song.

Tottenham had been tracking him for a couple of seasons, and with a pretty abysmal record in such matters failed to recognise that his first touch lacked the finesse for the highest echelons of the game, and snapped him up before the start of the 2003–04 season. In spite of the investment of time and money it was not too long before they realised they had bought a turkey, and with only a solitary goal in meaningful action for Tottenham, he was rapidly (well six months later to be exact) offloaded as a "makeweight" in a deal that would lead to Jermaine Defoe coming to White Hart Lane. A more talented twenty-one year old, whose popularity at Upton Park had plummeted when he wasted no time in making his feelings known about West Ham being relegated: quite simply the "Nationwide" was beneath him. Everyone believed that he was on his way to Old Trafford. Word was that it was a done deal, so it was a considerable surprise to many that he came to Tottenham. Rather like the "Sol Campbell" affair at Tottenham the sense of betrayal amongst the West Ham faithful was hard to avoid. To lose one of one's better players to the "Tottscum" was unbearable. Collective depression deepened when news filtered through that Defoe had opened his Tottenham account within fifteen minutes of his debut. David Thomas had trekked up to Bradford (some places always have that quality to them) and he was at Valley Parade approximately an hour later to enjoy Zamora (restored to the level at which he could prosper) rattling in his first goal for his new club. The immediate response from West Ham's travelling support, this time to the tune of "Volare", and sung with commendable gusto, was "Zamora oh-oh/ Zamora woah-oh-oh-oh/ He comes from White Hart Lane/ He's better than Jermaine/ Zamora". Maybe Jung was onto something with his "collective unconscious" stuff, for the player concerned had been at the club for less than a week—where *did* that song come from?

Freud was most certainly intrigued by such matters, and on the subject of telepathy he mused on the possibility of a process whereby "a mental act in one person would instigate the same mental act in another person". Sounds pretty much like that singing to me. He proposed "an original archaic method of communication between individuals", suggesting that we might get some clue from "the common purpose . . . in the great insect communities", "in passionately excited mobs" (the nearest he came to writing anything about football), or yet again in "the mental life of children". Psychoanalysis so often enjoying the metaphor of the child in the adult—the faintly nauseating "child within".

But perhaps it is much to do with trance states or the dream space that football provides. The standard justification for hypnotherapy is that it aims to entice the mind of the person under treatment (and curiously we can do it to ourselves) to turn inwards and connect with deeper levels of consciousness. More habitually these are unavailable, hence they are conventionally referred to as the unconscious. The story goes (for as with all of these ideas they are always only stories amongst stories, which is in no way to dilute their significance) that it is "in" the unconscious that all the real choices that one makes are made. Including whether one is more or less healthy or sick. The idea is that if you can induce someone to enter this realm, you have them optimally poised for healing, whether the symptoms are principally physical or psychological. The irony of this is that it is our normal waking state that is actually the trance state, in a dulled faintly anaesthetised way. How else could we cope with walking down Oxford Street?

Winnicott thought that our more habitual state was to be mildly depressed, "except when we are on holiday" (or at the football). But the corollary of this is that what is more usually referred to as the trance state is actually the awakened state, an altered state of heightened awareness. It is what so many of us have attempted to arrive at via the insistent use of recreational drugs. (Football having become for so many the recreational drug of choice.) These are the words of a hypnotherapist, "You use trance techniques to break the trance you probably didn't even realise that you were in. Once you wake up from the trance of the everyday into the deeper, more *universally* cognisant state, your vision literally brightens, your relationship with reality takes on a whole new perspective and your *ease of communicating* increases exponentially". So maybe, just maybe, those moments of collective telepathy and those occasional predictions that crop up in dreaming are all an effect of the altered state that football provides. Is that why, for certain politicians, football is recognised as "the opium of the people"?

Certainly it is nothing new for socio-political commentators to interpret football as a social anaesthetic, a form of diversion or emotional release that might otherwise emerge in the form of political protest. The theory is that under advanced capitalism the unfolding social conditions are such that the uprising of the underclasses is nigh on inevitable. Vinnani in his book *Football Mania* suggests that "the pseudoactivity of football canalises the energies which could shatter the existing power structures". The narrative that follows is one of devious public-school educated men who spotted a simple way of keeping the factory floor out of mischief, or out of the pub fermenting political unrest: get the workers out on the park and playing football. These ex-public school boys were now industrial moguls and their enthusiasm for the game had emerged at school. After all the early FA Cup finalists in the late nineteenth century were invariably Old Etonians, Old Carthusians, Oxford University and the like, so it was a natural extension of the bosses' paternalism to turn to football as an answer to what to do "when Saturday comes". By 1885 this "capitalist plot" had become so successful that football playing workers started to create their own industry: football became a business and players started to get paid to play.

Professional football was off and running, and the Old Boys clubs of the "old school" were consigned to the backwater of the Amateur Football Alliance. Perhaps inevitably other workers began to link themselves to the emerging clubs of their locality, and the age of the football fan began. As did the construction of stadia. All over the place and all occasioning a considerable up welling of civic pride, and of course this continues to this day with the ceremonial pomp attending the inauguration of another new ground, whether it be in Korea and Japan for the 2002 World Cup, or the more local, prosaic variety.

As with drugs (but unlike sex) the first time is almost invariably the best time when it comes to experiencing a sports venue. As Simon Inglis writes in his incomparable *The Football Grounds of England and Wales* "anyone who has been to a football match will know the rush of excitement when first catching sight of the floodlights and stands". For me it was on a grim March afternoon stumbling through the cramped, dark turnstile off an inner-city backstreet, and the hit was immediate. The waterfall rush of terracing that to a 14-year-old's eyes seemed to go on forever, and then the pure shimmering highlight, that sacred space, that green: the pitch. That can only have been a halluci-nation as by March in the 1950s there would have been precious little grass left. Then the eye-catching "Supporters Club" picked out in large lettering on the side of a building perched high up beside the main stand, neat, compact, all woodwork, pitched roof and glass screens; a few industrial icons of pylons and factory chimneys, and that was it—hooked. Welcome to League Football. For me it was Vicarage Road. Watford FC.

But I digress. The socialist theory runs as follows: whilst there were no gains in physical fitness from the watching of football at least it went some way towards keeping the workers engrossed. The industrial bosses in turn became the directors of the football clubs, and grand club traditions were developed in all the major industrial centres in Europe. Again, pursuing the psychoanalytic insistence on the words used, much emphasis is placed on the language of praise for a "good player". So often congratulations stressed "high work rate", "covering every blade of grass on the pitch", "getting stuck in", "not shirking tackles", all underpinning the representation of the "player" as "worker". Emblematic of this ethic might well be Alan Shearer, in appearance so reminiscent of those Soviet posters idealising the pasty-faced pre-war factory worker.

Thus the emphasis tended towards work rather than play, thereby underlining the capitalist work-ethic even during the rest and recuperation of the workers' leisure hours. Put at its most blunt this theory has it that the development of modern day football has always already been a—conscious or otherwise— bourgeois-capitalist scheme aimed at seducing the workers, under the light anaesthetised charm of a game, to keep their minds on the glory of hard work and well away from the pub and any thoughts of political fomentation. The highly competi- tive, high energy quality of football took care of the first, and the collective loyalty marinated in waves of intense excitement dealt with the latter. Although they all went down the pub anyway. The difficulty of this analysis is that it consistently overestimates the collective intelligence of the boss class whilst underestimating that of the workers, who hardly had football foisted on them passively. Rather, they clamoured for it, entirely active in organising and promoting it. Arthur Hopcraft in his marvellous 1968 classic *The Football Man* sought to explain the importance of the game in English life, "The working class saw it as an escape out of drudgery, and claimed it as their own . . . the game lives like an extra pulse in the people of industrial England". That low technology, labour-intensive factory-floor experience informed the way that football was played and appreciated. Teamwork, dependability and an emphasis on physical strength all played their part whether it was down the mines or out on the football field. Despite all the evident social changes that have taken place since the Second World War: the impact of television, the money, the new stadia and the influx of foreign players, to name just a few from the world of football, something adheres, something of these traditional virtues sticks. Back to Shearer as enduring icon of the contemporary game—at least here in England.

And perhaps here is yet another clue as to the sustained appeal of football. Set in the context of Europe's aspirant Americanisation—the Bluewater effect—football goes some way towards providing some reassuring contact with the imaginary and disappearing world of industrial society. Rather in the way that the long running soap *Coronation Street* took off at roughly the same time as the demolition boys moved in on much of Manchester. Our dreams marinated in the maternal reassurance of the half time Bovril. The idea that football seeps into everything gains a little momentum when one learns that *Coronation Street* was based on an actual street in Salford, as depicted in the famous rooftops shot in the opening title sequence, and that a Manchester United player, Eddie "Snake Hips" Colman, who died in the Munich air crash, was brought up in "Elsie Tanner's house".

Talking of "Snake Hips" an entirely different story unfolds in South America, where no doubt Starbucks is gearing up for complete market dominance. Although linked to 20th century urban expansion, football in that continent is far less entangled with industrial sensibilities, partly an effect of the economic primacy of the exportation of raw materials, and partly to do with trace elements of feudal notions of prestige and hierarchy. As was the case pretty much everywhere football was introduced by the British but was re-interpreted by South Americans, adapting it with all the attendant international acclaim for those of stocky build and a low-slung centre of gravity. A feudal insistence on hierarchy is perhaps strongest in Brazil, certainly in football terms. There you will witness extraordinary machinations to preserve the entitlements of the traditional "giants", incorrigible reluctance to accept that even the so called "big" teams who finish bottom should be relegated. As if Fluminense in the second division would be somehow "unnatural". But we all know and enthuse over the Brazilian's skill on the ball, which unlike the seeming class solidarity of the English game, is upheld as intoxicating moments of individual brilliance, almost as if it is a form of being able to dribble mesmerically round the somewhat rigid rules of hierarchy. The Maradona who can, with a subtle shimmy, dump his opponent on the seat of his pants, is the serf, the slum kid who became king, the humiliated who now humiliates, thus living out the dream of so many. The articulation of defiance.

Some would claim that the greatest of them all was Garrincha, the name used in north east Brazil for a "wren", who even his fellow countryman Pele defers to. They played together fifty-seven times for Brazil and were never on a losing side (won fifty, drew seven). Almost as if out of a 1950s *D.C. Thompson* comic (anyone recall "Limpalong Leslie"?), his right knee bent inwards, his left splayed outwards, he had a dislocated hip, was only 5ft 6ins tall and weighed in at ten stone, and according to the numerous women in his life he had a ten-inch penis. But let us concentrate on his football. Lodged in the TV archives in Sao Paulo is some extraordinary footage which reveals his incorrigible talent: playing for Botafogo he is out, as usual, on the right wing with the ball at his feet with the full back bearing down on him ready to pounce. Suddenly Garrincha sprints down the touchline with the defender in hot pursuit. Garrincha stops and we see that the ball has remained where it was. Untouched. He returns to the ball, and stands perfectly still for a few seconds before, once again he is darting down that wing. Again dragging the increasingly exasperated opponent with him. Again the ball never moves, and again Garrincha almost ambles back to stand over the ball with the defender resuming his vigil. But the third time the full back is rooted doggedly to the spot as Garrincha, yet again, shoots off down that wing. Only this time with the ball.

In Brazil he was known as "Joy of the People". All style and panache, fulfilling their dreams. Idolised. There was a time when such players would fill stadia all over South America, whilst now—as an effect of that export imperative and the seductions of Europe, attendances, particularly in Brazil, are in sorry decline. Which is not to say that football is any less popular, judging by the explosions of Sao Paulo street ecstasies when Brazil scooped up yet another World Cup in Yokohama in 2002.

It is this issue of ecstasy and its link to dream space that I want now to take up. It is said that we can never get to the dream itself, there is only ever dreaming and the retrieval of reconstructed trace elements. Just like the game, there is only ever playing or watching that playing, and the archiving of traces, memory traces. We are always in the place of the elusive, however many video replays we may bombard ourselves with. Freud was always quick to point to the navel of the dream, a stain of insistent opacity that will always elude capture. The specificity of any particular game, as with "the dream", will come from nowhere, only to disappear behind itself.

For the French philosopher Baudrillard the fundamental dynamic of our being is seduction. We are only at our most alive when seduced, carried away, taken over by whatever it may be: a particular smile, a piece of music, a passage of play. For the New York psychoanalyst Michael Eigen it is ecstasy that is at the heart of us, and it is linked to a radiance, to light. His claim is that there is an ecstatic core both at the heart of psychoanalysis and life itself. It is a term which is linked to the mystical, to love, to the poetic, and it is what drives our love . . . of football. But paradoxically, or one might claim dialectically, it is linked to the most excruciating state: to agony. And let us recall that for Huizinga it was agony that was his crucial term: to struggle, to agonise is right there at the heart of play. You cannot have one without the other. Of course when it comes to football so often one man's ecstasy is embedded in another's catastrophic dismay.

Mourinho's whooping, flapping vulture dance of joy along the Old Trafford touchline early on in 2004 following that last minute goal simultaneously thrust a dagger into the dreams of Ferguson, his team and all United followers. Crucial goals will inevitably trigger moments of transfiguring delirium, uncontainable upwellings of ecstasy, which may so often be twinned with the exultations of vengeful rage and an envying torrent. The anticipation of such moments creates the suspense. A particularly well humoured response to being on the receiving end of such raucous outpourings came from the young ferret faced Tottenham fan, perched high up on a plinth-like structure gazing out over Wembley Way. It was a Sunday early in April 1993. Another semi-final had just finished. The street was chock full of baying, chortling Arsenal fans, all on their way up to Wembley Park tube station after their 1–0 win had gone some way towards revenging that sour defeat in a previous Wembley semi-final two years earlier. With an amused, almost proprietorial gaze accompanied by a large grin he shouted out at the Arsenal fans, "Go on then! Fucking MILK IT!" An unconscious recognition of triumph as dream screen, dream scene as breast.

For Eigen ecstasy is "in the blood", a term that is so often used by fans as if it in some way formed a coherent explanation with regard to their attachment to a particular side ("Why the Albion?" "It's in the blood"). The blood-soul-ecstasy bond is as old as the hills, and football is no exception. Metaphorically the smell of blood, going for the kill are deeply suffusing the game. As is well documented football has been played in England for hundred of years. Initially it was a game played by unruly clusters of men and boys all deliriously charging down lanes and across fields, always anarchic, almost always invariably a violent free-for-all, with serious injuries not uncommon. Inevitably the authorities attempted to outlaw it but the tradition and basic will of the people to let off steam in this particular form had its way. An infamous contest evolved between two local parishes in Derby, taking place well into the middle of the nineteenth century every Shrove Tuesday and Ash Wednesday. It involved literally hundreds of "players" all urged on by countless onlookers, and it was from this that the term "local derby" arose. This is Eigen, "Twist the sense of power and you have the frenzy of Nazi calculation ... exultation in exterminating ecstasies." Clearly one does not have to kill or maim to discover ecstasy and yet listen to those howls from the terraces—"Put the nails in" (as in batten down the coffin lid), another goal will "kill 'em off", will destroy all hope of recovery. And all this is marinated in love, love of ecstasy.

For many there is no greater passion, and that imperative to love with all one's soul and all one's might, almost operating as a command, carries so many away. The Freudian notion of "free association", the psychic act of relinquishing, as far as is possible, any slavish devotion to internal censors, operates as a testimony to ecstasy. Again Eigen, "The call ignites striving, grows out of tasting the great striving. It gathers power, attracting other strivings into its orbit or current, barely leaving room for dissidents." Football fans on an awayday, rampaging down to the ground. It is a striving that feeds on fighting and surrender. A striving so linked to that moment of transfiguring rapture, a striving for a ... GOAL. What else was going on, or in the vernacular, "kicking off", in Derby on those Tuesdays and Wednesdays?

So within these ecstasies there is always this accompanying potential for agony. For some the idealisation of the love tie is merely a defence against the writer Milan Kundera's "unbearable lightness of being" or Lacan's insistence on the grotesque lack that saturates our soul. Football is so often referred to as the "beautiful game" but for Lacan an emphasis on beauty invariably veils an unbearable yet foundational horror. We come in to the world mutilated by loss and are driven to redress this via dream. The food, the milk (you are never far away from the breast in psychoanalysis) that supports life, that moves in the direction of satisfaction allows us to dream. The infant sleeps blissfully. And we dream to keep on sleeping. Dreams nourish our being, our spirits and feed our psyche, but always, just round the corner, there is the crushing awakening of loss, defeat. You cannot be a football person without a thorough acquaintance of what Eigen refers to as "black hole ecstasies". These are sites of catastrophic dismay, damage, and incommutable injustice. In part this intermingling of agony and ecstasy allows a filtering of such experiences, allows a flow of illusion and disillusion, all marinated in anxiety. In part we are on the edge of our seats, at the edge of heart-wrenching disappointment so entangled with the twisted passion for ecstasy. An ecstasy that may turn round the deprivation of the other of the spoils, that in-mixing of relief ecstasy at the moment of the last minute equaliser. Or up at Old Trafford in the autumn of 2003, the moment of that missed penalty.

It is impossible to be around football for any length of time without coming up against those infamous words of Bill Shankly that were touched on in the introduction: "Some people think that football is a matter of life and death. I'm very disappointed by that attitude. I can assure you that it is much, much more important than that." And at times it can be hard to avoid some of the faint trails of explanations: that he wasn't entirely serious, not really, only joking, or that it was merely the psychosis inducing effect of the amphetamines he was doling out in the Carlisle dressing room. So on and so forth. All in a wan attempt to justify what appears so manifestly absurd. Almost as many readings as generated by Freud and his case history of Dora and the lakeside kiss. Following Dostoevsky a dying child is an evil that lacerates philosophical beauty: goodness dies when a child dies. Can we not all agree, how can the mere loss of a game of football be in any way comparable? Surely we are at the site of a massive (to the point of delusional) misidentification? It is as if we are entangled in an absurd loss of perspective, for to lose a game of football is hardly a tragedy. Worse things happen in life, a lot worse.

At times it can become horrifying to acknowledge how important football has become. It is out of all proportion. On occasions it is all somewhat rather akin to the anguish and exquisite joys of the transferential tie. Transference in this instance has no link whatsoever with transfers or transfer fees, but is the psychoanalytic term for the particularly heightened state of emotional involvement the "patient" has with his or her analyst. Such moments are linked to a potential for horrified self recognition, for what may be revealed is something that is deeply true: that so much passion is devoted to something that is basically trivial. This can be a maddening realisation: the revelation that all this is incredibly banal. We meet up with the lack of the profound set against the infinite complexities and contradictions of our life, and yet is this not precisely what is so embedded in the attractions of football? It is part of its enduring allure. For what we may note is that such realisations, perhaps like a whole host of psychoanalytic interpretations, have little to no effect. They wash over us. It is hardly that there is a sense of reconciliation, an acceptance of our insistent superficiality. Rather, without hesitation we are swept up, once more swallowed up by its unrelenting intensities. Football rarely lets go. The same goes for psychoanalysis, at least in some shape or form, for although the involvement with a particular analyst may fade (indeed let us hope so) involvement with psychoanalysis as a body of ideas is less easy to shake off. Freud's ideas about the "death drive", which is so often referred to as the compulsion to repeat, is that something is lost, a bit of us dies, some particular energy disappears. And it is terminal, we never "recover", for we are possessed, condemned to return over and over again. To do it again. The content will never repeat but the foundational structures are immutable. To keep on dreaming. Ecstasy is always just round the corner.

And part of what we dream of is belonging. Much of this is linked to recognition; recognition not as in the capacity to differentiate between different team shirts, different players, but recognition as inclusion, the arm around the shoulder, inclusion in the community. This is the football photographer Stuart Clarke in his *More Than a Match: The Homes of Football*, "Whereas my brother, as most, watched every footballing move, I have always looked sideways . . . or through the crack of the door. I love as much the atmosphere of the big ground and the big game . . . my other home, a glorious ridiculous home from home: the football ground." One of the enduring attractions of football is that it is hard to think of quite what else in our world has that peculiar capacity to unite people across so many different national—or here in Britain class—boundaries, to provide this home from home. An egalitarian home. It has always been a game of the masses, and has continually offered a level playing field for the poorer members of any community. It is difficult to imagine another walk of life where those not only of African descent but also coming from other less economically advantaged communities are so subject to admiration and acclaim. It bears repetition that it can never be simply a matter of kicking a ball about for not only does it have the capacity to arouse passion beyond the rational, but can manifestly affect the mood of nations, even to the point of shifting the fortunes of governments. It allows whole nations to dream. Football is one of the great universal experiences, for wherever you are in the world there is always football. As my family has come to recognise.

And it permits the dream of belonging. Some years ago I was in Antwerp when it was the European Capital of Culture. My wife and I had done the cultural things: the galleries, the dock architecture, the fashion outlets for the Antwerp Six, the restaurants, the bars. And all very pleasurable it was too. But always as the outsider, the visitor, the tourist. On the Friday evening I am rattling along the dimly lit streets out to the suburbs in a rickety tram, and I feel different. There are a smattering of cheerful, red-faced locals, some with football scarves on, naturally enough they are all chatting away in Flemish, and I am completely ignored. But the difference is that just for that moment I feel included, I too belong, am part of the community that find a little excursion out to the cramped little ground of Beerschot utterly irresistible. It brings a smile to my face, and one or two shyly smile back.

Of course there are the people who are utterly impervious. The onslaught of television coverage and the bombardment in our newspapers leaves many unmoved, who see an interest in a mere game as compelling evidence of arrested development—for so many of us precisely its charm. Like those of us who boast about "being hopeless at maths" as if this ignorance is in some way virtuous—they seldom miss an opportunity to hold forth on how absolutely uninformed they are when it comes to sport, and couldn't tell Alex Ferguson from Ian Botham. They are welcome to their impoverished view, their impossible snobbery that merely reveals their inability to recognise the whole. The whole world in which sport takes its place along with the political, along with science and industry and art. And psychoanalysis. Nobody has put it better than Arthur Hopcraft in his book *The Football Man*. He wrote "The point about football in Britain (and this could just as easily refer to the whole wide world) is that it is not just a sport people take to, like cricket or tennis or running long distances. *It is inherent in the people* [my emphasis]. It is built into the urban psyche, as much a common experience to our children as are uncles and school. It is not a phenomenon: it is an everyday matter. There is more eccentricity in deliberately disregarding it than in devoting a life to it. Its sudden withdrawal from the people would bring deeper disconsolation than to deprive them of television. The way we play the game, organise and reward it reflects the kind of community we are." The unimaginable: a life without football. Certainly destined to outlive psychoanalysis.

Crucially once people are caught up in playing who they are or where they come from ceases to be of concern. All that counts is "Can he/she play?" Whether a psychoanalyst or a printer, a Frenchman or a Kiwi, difference is effaced for the duration of the game. This is an effect of all being caught up and carried away in playing the same game with the result that all hierarchies are dissolved. And the same goes for watching: a country's president is for a particular moment simultaneously as engrossed, as equally caught up in rapture, as any of the other spectators. Whether it is barefoot on African sand or punting a beer can around the back streets of Budapest all can belong, all can be included, each according to their abilities. The one chipping the cross over can do that wherever they are in the world, and whilst acknowledging considerable variations in styles of play one thing is for sure: a good goal is a good goal is a good goal anywhere. Always exhilarating. Exuberance rules.

Many of us may have dreamed of playing in the great stadia of the world, me included. One year one of my sides, *the Times*, had got to the final of the Fleet Street Mid-Week League Cup, the opposition was *the Sun*, and it was all set for us to play a "pipe opener" before one of the play offs over the Whit weekend under the twin towers at Wembley. The father of one of our players had even booked a flight down from Scotland to see his boy play. But it was not to be: a couple of days before we were due to play it was decided that, "owing to excessive wear and tear of the playing surface", our match would be shifted to Craven Cottage. Cue considerable wailing and gnashing of teeth. I now console myself that at least it was fun to have got that close, for after all the "universal" experience is hardly one of perfectly tended pitches and immaculately matching socks. In so many cases the conditions may be verging on the adverse: Peruvian floodlit car parks to corrugatedly rutted recreation grounds may be much more the order of the day. But football, as with dreaming, allows a transcendence of the surroundings. Football is football is football as those photographs of the Iraqi Premier-ship still in full flow with the backdrop of the burning oilfields soon after war had broken out bear testimony. People and football are people and football the world over. We just live in different conditions.

The French existentialist Jean Paul Sartre had this to say about football, ". . . in a match everything is complicated by the pre-sence of the opposite team". The same goes for psychoanalysis, for all the theories are complicated by the presence of the one sitting opposite (or lying on the couch or what have you). And it is always only a one off. This is true for our dreams, even those that seem to be the same. Note that we only ever use that word "same" when already more than one is in play, when there is already difference. At the beginning of the 2004–05 season I found myself by the bus stop outside White Hart Lane idly and pleasurably arguing with a small group of Liverpool supporters about Michael Owen's departure to Real Madrid. Psychoanalysis wants to claim that we will all have a tendency to denigrate what we have lost, as a defence against the sadness. The sadness so often linked to a rupturing of our dreams. One of the Liverpool supporters was insisting that the departure of Owen was no great loss, buttressing his argument with the claim that Owen's goal against Portugal in the quarter-final of Euro 2004 had been a fluke. A fluke to me has always meant that it wasn't meant. But the Liverpool fan was insistent: he could never do it again, he couldn't repeat it. And of course he was right. In the World Cup Final in Rome in 1934 Italy were trailing 1–0 with ten minutes to go. Raimondo Orsi suddenly burst into the Czechoslovakian penalty area, feinted to shoot with his left foot but unleashed a superb equaliser with his right, and Italy went on to lift the trophy. The next morning Orsi was summoned to the vaingloriously titled Stadio del Partido Nacional Fascista to try and recreate that sublime moment for the benefit of the assembled press photo-graphers. No opposition to hinder him or to complicate matters, yet after over twenty attempts all gave up and headed off for lunch. Owen's goal was no fluke but it was unrepeatable.

There is something about this singularity, this unrepeatability that is so crucial. It is far from uncommon when somebody discovers what I do to earn a living to be asked "But don't you get fed up, listening to the same stories over and over again?". But the stories are never the same, and on the occasions when it appears as if they are, it is because something is not being heard. One is being called to listen from a different place. And for so many of us something of a similar order operates in relation to football. One never tires of it. Both football and psychoanalysis are interminable. Possibly the essential universal element that lurks in the midst of the dream space is not only that hunger, that unquenchable desire for ecstasy, but also that which we all share: the human body.

Maybe it is a generational thing but almost invariably whenever a ball is produced, and it can be a silly looking multicoloured tiny tot's plastic one, the effect is the same. Up goes the cry "Put one on me bonce". Possibly the more contemporary phrase will be "On me 'ead, son", if the *Hamlet* cigar advert is anything to go by. Framing this moment is the dream of the sublime, the longed-for moments of exquisite grace, the leaping— like a salmon—to head the ball emphatically into the imaginary net, all so entangled in the feel of the human body in motion. Folded into this is the quest for style, which is another word for cool. For some the one who most epitomises this quality is the fleet footed va-va-voom man Thierry Henry. When he slips into overdrive the heart leaps. For another generation it was "Kaiser" Beckenbauer seemingly effortlessly and so elegantly stepping out of defence, and before then there was the incomparable Danny Blanchflower, described by his Tottenham team mate Dave Mackay as "having style in everything he did on the field. He could look stylish standing still."

What more could any of us dream of?

Sex in the Stadium

reud came up with a particular form of therapy called psychoanalysis, which was and continues to be a particular form of thinking about the workings of our minds. To a considerable extent he was able to elucidate something of the sexual aspects not only of the "innocence" of our childhoods, but so often on the basis of an examination of our dream life, he arrived at his foundational emphasis on the unconscious forces or drives that influence our everyday thoughts and actions. And this emphasis was founded on the sexual. Inevitably other thinkers in the field demurred, Jung for example wanting to place spirituality at the heart of our being. More recently and perhaps more interestingly the French cultural theorist Baudrillard joined the queue of those ultimately more dismissive of the potential reductionism in the thesis that the basis of our being is sexual. For Baudrillard seduction is the key.

Nevertheless let us pursue the idea, so incontrovertibly associated with Freud, that there is something that he sought to call sexuality at the heart of everything. Not so much in terms of whether this is true or not, but as a rhetorical device, as something that would promote a thinking. Or more importantly an enjoyment. The importance no longer residing in whether a particular set of ideas is true or not, but whether we derive anything much through allowing their possibility.

According to Freud's terms we are by and large unconscious of so much that informs what goes on between people, that so structures the way we are together and yet plays such a part in keeping us at a distance. Sexuality is seen as being the coinage of exchange between people, or as Adam Phillips puts it in his introduction to Freud's *Wild Analysis*, "It is the satisfaction that we seemed to suffer, and the suffering that seemed to satisfy . . ."

It is a moot point as to whether the incontestable fact that Freud's ideas regarding the Oedipus complex—that everyone's original goal was the forbidden object or objective of incestuous desire—are now so ubiquitous, so ultimately commonplace, operates as testimony to their incontrovertible truth. For why else would we be so taken by such a story, yet we might allow that something more complex, more insidious is in play. But whatever we may make of this, one thing is for sure: Freud was engaged in a radical disruption or re-description of our basic goals. Rather than a pursuit of the "Good life" (which is to be understood in its original, more ethical sense, and not to be conflated with a world of birds, booze, cars and cocaine of *Footballers' Wives* sensibilities), Freud insists on these "objects" of forbidden desire. These turn up only too early in our lives. They are foundational even—will never let go, even if our ways of seeking them out may pass through a whole host of paths of indirection. Through paths of dissociation, of distortion, of condensation, all an effect of censorship.

And one of the things about football is that clearly it turns around, the whole shebang hinges on this term "goal". That primary objective. At the same time it sustains, however indirectly, a form of umbilical link to the so called "innocence" of our childhood. This, following Freud, is now to be recognised as saturated with sexuality, with all that trails in its wake in terms of issues of gender and sexual difference. And one of the things that is hard to miss is how sexual terms bleed effortlessly into the vocabulary of football. Thus inviting the thought that there must be some connection. But in what way precisely?

Of course we are all subject to the insistence that we grow up. We are all supposed to "mature", which appears to have a considerable amount to do with a suppression of childish interests. We are called upon to compromise these interests. And in part it looks as if those interests are sexual. After all there are lots of questions about it early on in our life, and it is difficult not to notice how assiduously we as children hang onto the theories that we have formed about the so called "facts of life". Above all children appear naturally sensuous, endlessly curious about sensation, about their bodies and about sex. All along the lines of what goes into and what comes out of where. Yet we are all subject to certain limits and limitations, effects of what Freud called "the ideals of education". It is these ideals that lead us along other divergent paths, paths of compromise. The oedipal narrative of wanting to be inside one's mother and wanting to kill off one's father runs deep, as if the basic, base even, interests of the child are somehow unacceptable. And it is here that we come up against the Freudian notion of sublimation.

The idea, which is notoriously difficult to pin down, certainly with regard to how it works, is fundamentally one of substitution. In the place of the forbidden longing we find some other satisfaction. This is the way that our desires slip through the barricades of censorship. When a desire cannot be represented consciously it can take on some form of the absurd, like a fish riding a bike in a dream (or in a stout advertisement). Jacques Lacan, whilst giving one of his sold out seminars, was touching on this subject of sublimation when he appealed to his audience, "Does this look as if I am fucking?" At one level absurd, but now he comes to mention it . . .

And initially it may seem absurd to suggest that football is a disguised way of having sex, but perhaps, here too, we might have second thoughts. Freud in his *Civilised Sexual Morality and Modern Nervous Illness* is never less than emphatic. Our sexual behaviour will more often than not lay down the basic patterning of all our other modes of reacting to life. So sex is taken as a template for how we engage with a whole host of seemingly quite different activities. And football will be no exception. According to Freud all those primordial interests that so informed our early childhood are going to find themselves diverted, redirected, displaced and channelled into more socially accepted activities. Rather than fucking in the streets we will end up punting a ball around, ultimately trying to ram it into the equivalent of a hole. And such diversions are called sublimations.

The idea originally stemmed from the world of chemistry and was a term used to denote transformation. This was brought about through "subliming", or converting a solid mass into a vapour, invariably by heat, which then re-solidifies upon cooling down. Psychoanalysis promotes the idea of something otherwise known as our forbidden desires hotting up only to be reconfigured in a cooler, condensed state. Our sexual and murderous desires have to be somehow "vaporised" only to re-emerge as something else, with those original desires now effectively concealed. Effectively chilled. Quite how this works is left suitably vague. The American psychoanalyst Donald Kaplan described it as "a vagrant problem for psychoanalysis". It always was and continues to be so. Another commentator on this idea, Hans Loewald, thought that we are all entangled in this illusory concealment. We just cannot avoid it, all intimately engaged in an intriguingly fanciful embellishment of our elementary instinctual and unconscious life. And without doubt certain aspects of football culture unequivocally involve something being kept hidden, something being suppressed. An illusory concealment. The elephant in the sitting room.

Until quite recently much of psychoanalysis, or at least in its institutional or organisational formations, was pretty much like every dressing room in the land: homophobia was stinking the place out. In other words a curious little enclave existed—or as far as football is concerned—not so little, in which no-one was gay. Statistically somewhat improbable, but it was cultured out nevertheless. Note that at international tournaments it is always "wives and girlfriends" that players are allowed to see by indulgent managers. It was not so long ago that people seeking to undergo a training in psychoanalysis would occasionally write embarrassingly coy articles in the professional journals. These, often operating as little more than vanity publishing puffs, were where it would be possible to find descriptions of, almost as acts of reassuring heroism, multiple forms of self-denial. All in the cause of slipping past the pathology police sitting on the respective training committees.

The one footballer who had the balls (see how the vocabulary insists) to come out publicly with regard to his sexual orientation was Justin Fashanu, the former Nottingham Forest, Norwich City and England U-21 striker. He was subject to verbal abuse from his bully boy manager Brian Clough who referred to him as a "bloody poof", and was shunned by pretty much everyone, including the inexorable John Fashanu, his footballer-turned-TV-presenter brother, who has plenty of form for football related chicanery. Justin ended up hanging himself in a garage in London's East End. Then there is the curious case of Graham Le Saux, for so long the England and Chelsea left back. His career has been consistently dogged by "shirt-lifter" and "faggot" insults. Never more so than in the incident with Robbie Fowler, then at Liverpool, who incited Le Saux via gesturing with his hands and buttocks. Everybody "got" the reference, despite Le Saux's understandable insistence that he was a family man. But the contagious impression from both dressing rooms and the terraces appeared to be a reflection of his being a *Guardian* reader and a collector of antiques. The "queer" fella. Having a couple of 'A'levels probably did not help as it further differentiated him from the more stereotypical, less articulate, Jack-the-lad image so exemplified by the aforementioned Fowler. Any such deviation from the perceived norm seems to inevitably raise questions about your sexuality.

To spend any length of time in dressing rooms at any level of the game, or in the company of those who take up their place on the margins of the game, however legitimately, such as football writers and scouts, is to be, not so subtly but significantly, subject to this insistent homophobic anxiety. The actor Ben Price, who had a starring role in *Footballers' Wives*, in which interestingly he displayed bi-sexual proclivities, noticed how almost invariably the ex-pros who were involved in filming the football bits of the series, would, to a man, express a concern over the possibility that "people might think" that he was gay. All convinced that "to play a bisexual footballer might make people 'suspect' you." To turn a phrase, it is strikingly conspicuous that no one in the professional game appears willing to break the code of silence that surrounds this issue. No doubt for the reasons that it would only invite the Le Saux treatment and could seriously jeopardise potentially lucrative sponsorship deals. Although Le Saux himself appears to have fairly seamlessly slipped into a *Match of the Day* niche.

However the former Irish international Tony Cascarino, from the sanctuary of retirement and the chronicles of his compulsive womanising in his book *Full Time; The Secret Life of Tony Cascarino* (although we all know what psychoanalysis might have to say about the womanising) has been able to be quite explicit in his condemnation of football for being an unrelentingly "macho world", so crowded with male stereotypes and dripping with beautiful women. In that environment it would be daunting for anyone to say that they were different. He had been subject to considerable antagonism early on in his career as an effect of once being a trainee hairdresser. (Although a notoriety for serial missing of "sitters" might have also contributed to his difficulties.) To admit that that one was gay, especially when it had been assumed that you were heterosexual, could potentially lead to inordinate difficulties. Cascarino said that he would "find it inconceivable that any player can come out during his career because he will simply not be accepted in the dressing room."

All this is enormously curious in a sport that makes pin-ups of its heroes, where goal scoring celebrations involves "jumping" ones team mates, with a smothering of kisses so often thrown in for good measure. After all, what else could we think that is involved in so many of us spending our winter afternoons and evenings watching other men run around in silk shorts, if it was not homoerotic? So fondly gazing, so wanting to be those men. Indeed you do not have to be a psychoanalyst to allow such thoughts. Some, such as the broadcaster David Aaronovitch, have put forward the only too plausible idea that the phenomenon of "roasting", where a small number of men take it in turns to fuck a girl, usually in a smart inner-city hotel, is informed by the suppressed desire to have sex with each other. He wrote that "Men sharing a girl is, if you think about it, as gay as kissing on the lips after scoring a goal: it is a way to have sex with your comrades without actually touching them." One of the people who come to see me for analysis is an Arsenal season-ticket holder. At one moment in our conversations we were musing idly on the inevitable "psychic homosexuality" that pervades all pubs. Of course it is not that there are no women in pubs, or that men do not pick up women in such locations (or vice-versa), but that the "culture", or an old fashioned psychoanalytic term, the "psychic economy" crucially turns around what other men think. With enviable speed of thought he said "Ahah, that gives a different inflection to 'Going up the Arse' on a Saturday afternoon."

As was mentioned previously, certainly in psychoanalysis it is possible to note a shifting awareness whereby there is a less compulsive pathologising of homosexuality, and maybe, just maybe, football, albeit very tentatively, follows suit. Since 1989 there has been a thriving Gay Football Supporters' Network that has built up its own amateur leagues made up of principally all gay teams. There is also a team further up the Pyramid in the Middlesex County League called Stonewall where it has been possible to both play football and be openly gay. When they began in 1992 they were subject to wearisome jokes about being Queens of the South, whereas nowadays it seems that opposing teams either do not know or do not care that Stonewall FC are gay. Occasionally, according to Chairman Chris Worth, abuse will emerge during games, but usually as an effect of their outplaying the opposition whose only resort "is to call us poofs". Nevertheless the existence of all or mainly gay teams, and of a gay league only illustrates the marginalisation that football as a subculture persists in.

Almost invariably homophobia goes hand in hand with misogyny, and that too is all part of the free association of both "terrace" and dressing room. It's a "man's game" alright. It is a curious phenomenon that a significant number of the so-called football greats end up with serious alcohol problems, and on occasions violence towards their loved ones only too easily seems to seep into the mix. Perhaps there is something of the heady intoxications of actually playing that become almost impossible to replace, and this violence to both self and other is a way of attempting to silence and to conceal their own vulnerability and maternal dependency that football had managed to veil. As Jimmy Greaves said, "It wasn't the pressure of playing that made me start drinking heavily, it was probably the emptiness of not playing." Of not playing with other men, in a culture that is strictly boystown.

Mention has been made of Beckham, of course—how could it not? But of course the prototype for all this (indeed it could be justifiably claimed that he started it all) was the incomparable George Best. Such a curious surname given his status as arguably the finest player produced in Britain, certainly since 1945. Almost slight in stature he had the enormously appealing quality of fearlessness in the face of the most rugged defenders. Having made his Manchester United debut at seventeen he was European Footballer of the Year by the age of twenty-two. But by then he had moved from the sports pages to the front of magazines, had become a household name in households where football had no hold. He was the first footballer to be hired as a model, unless you count Denis Compton (not only an extraordinarily good cricketer) and the *Brylcreem* ads, and Stanley Matthews, who had been used to promote the merits of *Craven A* cigarettes. But for Best an extraordinary roller-coaster of possibilities beckoned. As Sean Hagen described "He was our style icon, our sex symbol and our pop star all rolled into one". Not quite the effect those cigarettes had for "our" Stan. Best was everybody's, could have every body, and was followed everywhere. Coach parties would arrive outside his new home in Cheshire merely to gawp at the tightly-drawn curtains. His hair, his clothes, his girlfriends, his delinquencies, his "lost" weekends, all unceasingly chronicled. He admitted that he used to go missing (Miss UK, Miss World . . .), and in his soft Belfast burr would mutter how if he had been born ugly "you'd never have heard of Pele." And for many there is as much fascination with his sex life as with his footballing exploits. But it was for his football that he was legendary. He had it all: coruscating pace, breathtaking courage, outrageous skill, sublime balance, and mesmeric invention. Johnny Tillotson had a hit in the 1950s with a song called *Poetry in Motion*. That was Best.

It might be said that he worked very hard to erode the legend, by his alcohol-fuelled behaviour, and the trail of wounded women left in the wake of his charmless and callous carelessness. Some would claim that he squandered his exceptional talent, and then followed through by squandering the opportunities he had for a new life. But despite the difficulties implicit in seeking to brush those caveats aside, something other insists. Something that football brings to the table. Something transcendent. There was something in his play that exemplifies the essential hold that football has: the capacity to inspire awe. It's rare, but he had it in uncontainable abundance. And you can get a whiff of it with Wayne Rooney. But back to Sean Hagen, for as he wrote, George Best was simply "forever brilliant, forever beautiful, forever young." Exquisitely distilling so much of what football has to offer. And perhaps in our dreams it is what sex can do for us too.

And whilst it is safe to say that David Beckham will never scale the footballing heights that Best attained, something of him as a sexual/sporting icon is replicated. Where the edges between sex and football become increasingly blurred. A description of he and Victoria getting it on in the back of their chauffeur–driven silver Bentley, having enjoyed a meal at London's Nobu restaurant, made reference to his "occupying his usual position on the right hand side" whilst she was enjoying the "central holding role". At some point she gained "control of his midfield with her foot", followed through and "with a gaping hole in his defence, she plunged towards goal, then clearly handled in the area". The *News of the World* reporters (Ray Singh and Hannah Perry) could not resist resorting to the old gag about "Becks being pulled off at half time", and the piece was suffused with references to "handball", "penalty area" and "hitting the target". It is not difficult to trace out the multiplicity of football terms that slip effortlessly into the common pool of ways of speaking about our relationships, particularly our sexual ones. And this is not limited to the unrelenting prose style of the tabloid newspaper. This is the *Observer*'s Kathryn Flett (their TV correspondent, albeit writing about a play—a TV drama about a footballer indulging himself in a bit of post match R&R date rape) ". . . this had been a game of two halves and plenty of scoring opportunities . . . in the face of a systematic attack on goal from Castlefield's star striker, her defence had completely disintegrated". Back and forth, football and sex and sex and football go. Swings both ways.

The crucial aim of the game is to score, which, in the English language at any rate, has unmistakable sexual connotations. So perhaps it is not so surprising that sex and sexual conquest simultaneously slides, at least in terms of vocabulary, into metaphors for describing how a team has "performed".

This is Ian Holloway, then manager of Second Division London club, Queens Park Rangers, describing his side's 3–0 win over Chesterfield one season, "To put it in gentleman's terms: if you have been out for a night and you're looking for a young lady and you pull one, some weeks they are good-looking and some weeks they're not the best. Our performance today would have been not the best-looking bird, but at least we got her in the taxi. She weren't the best-looking lady we ever ended up taking home, but she was very pleasant and very nice, so thanks very much, let's go and have a coffee."

And don't think for a moment that the spectators are left out of this. As I walk into our hotel foyer that doubled up as a small bar in Mexico City during the 1986 World Cup, having just flown in from Monterrey following England's somewhat dispiriting 1–0 defeat in their opening game, immediately I am met by an amiable Scotsman. He had previously befriended me and my travelling companion. With a consoling arm around my shoulder, and a conspiratorial whisper in my ear he says, "Do you know what? When that Portuguese goal went in, I nearly came in my pants." He had been waiting all evening for that moment.

Another story from the consulting room involved another Arsenal fan. He had been musing over the Nick Hornby emphasis on football becoming the medium of communication between father and son in lieu of an otherwise potential abyss of awkwardness. This had not been the case for this particular man and his dad for they had got along pretty well. His father had been living in Finland in the 1930s and had followed English football from afar. Arsenal under Herbert Chapman, having reeled off three consecutive Championships during this period, was to become the team of choice. Almost inevitably, having come to live in London the father started to go to a few games, and at a certain age decided it was time to introduce his son to the delights of the North Bank. A generation on, the son, now a father in his own right, felt moved to do the same with his boy who was only seven. Initially it all went horribly wrong with his son finding it all too frightening and so they both left early. Undeterred he took him along two years later. And this time the magic worked, "Just the same as me, it hit him right between the legs", and it was this phrase that caught the attention. Rather akin to the phrase "living for kicks" it proposes an incorrigible link between pleasure and pain. Genital anguish and ecstasy. Incidentally the son, now a grown man, rings his father to tip him off about how to get into the ground on the cheap, to punt a madcap scheme. Both fully embroiled not only with each other but with feeding the addiction.

A term of denigration for someone who has had a poor game is the inevitable "wanker", and very occasionally a player may deflect disapproval by ironising this. I remember Alan Mullery, playing for Tottenham, having ballooned a shot over the bar, peeling away making the "wanker" gesture to none other than himself, thus stifling the imminent groans and transforming the crowd's antagonism into a collective rueful grin. Scoring a goal becomes the climax of a particular passage of play, and with this goes the insistent association with orgasm, of "bursting the net". It is commonplace for players to draw attention to this with inevitable comparisons. "Almost as good as" or "better than sex". Beckham, ever the gentleman, always gets his priorities right. Ryan Giggs, for so long Beckham's team mate at Old Trafford, is more diffident, "Gazza said that scoring was better than an orgasm. Lee Chapman reckoned that it wasn't as good. I'll go with Pele—he thought that it was about the same."

The etymology of the word goal is intriguing if somewhat obscure. The first evidence of the word "gol" appears in England in 1314 meaning a "boundary marker", a limit. But the theory is that this stemmed from the Olde English "gal", from the verb "galen" which meant to "sing, cry out or celebrate", as if it all derives from connotations of joy and abandon. An orgasmic insistence.

Immediately following the scoring of a goal both players and spectators are instantaneously carried away into an explosion of what Desmond Morris calls the "triumph display". For players it has become increasingly difficult to find something sufficiently idiosyncratic that will differentiate them for the more usual routines. Morris traces this out via a differentiation of the two phases, at least for the players: the reaction of the scorer and the response of his team mates. Typically the scorer may take off on a wild careering run, sometimes but not necessarily ending up in the proximity of the team dugout. Morris sees this as driven by the need for a release of tension. As a form of multiple orgasm of overflowing, uncontainable euphoria, as well as a wish to deflect any suggestion that the scorer is waiting to be congratulated. The latter thesis is a little more problematic as so often the scorer appears to have embarked on a wilful call to play "catch me if you can", with what Morris refers to as "the embrace invitation". Another standard response is the raised arm with hand variations: the "hail Caesar", the tight fist "power to the people", the single pointing finger, or the Denis Law trademark: the red-sleeved arm with the clutched cuff, are the usual. Tottenham's Gus Poyet added to the repertoire with the finger over his lips, having scored in the last minute, to "shush" his detractors who had been less than enthusiastic when he was introduced for the last quarter of an hour of a 4–3 humdinger against Portsmouth. Here the emphasis is more on the reaction to the acclaim of the crowd. Other reactions involve the full raising of both arms which has the effect of making the scorer seem larger and taller. The player may describe himself as feeling "ten feet tall" or more typically as "over the moon", jumping up and waving a fist, punching the air. Giving it the large.

Now psychoanalysis might, if it were less cautious in never wishing to stray from the specificity of the *words*, engage in *analysing* the peculiarities of particular player's celebratory tics: Mick Channon's whirling arm, Robbie Keane's cartwheels culminating in the cowboy gunslinger pose or Thierry Henry and his sprint to the corner flag, to stand erect, frowning, quivering, biting his lip. It is the latter who drew forth a particularly inventive piece of sustained analysis, as follows: he is compulsively driven, at this moment of his own personal glory, to enact the "trembling" efforts of his compatriots during the Second World War who so conspicuously "rolled over" in the face of the Nazi invasion. This spontaneous gesture of (feigned) contrition operates as strong evidence that he spends his close season back on his native soil engaged in grave desecration of (British) war heroes in various parts of Normandy. As is so often the case the "psychoanalytic" interpretation often says every bit as much about the analyst—in this instance a Leeds fan who had just witnessed a grave dereliction of duty as his side had "rolled over" in the face of repeated Arsenal attacks—as it does about the person under investigation. But here you might glimpse a brilliant instance of the unfettered or "wild analysis" that appeared to so vex Freud and his followers, until things were tightened up a bit. (See Jacqueline Rose's admirable introduction to *Jacques Lacan and the Question of Psychoanalytic Training* by Moustapha Safouan for further elaboration of such concerns.)

For psychoanalysis, or at least among certain schools of thought, the "moment of truth", the goal that is searched after, is the moment of the "correct interpretation". Whilst for others this is wildly overestimated. In football it is that putting the ball in the back of the net that counts—although of course there does not literally have to be a net. In medieval folk-football the goal was an object or a place that the ball had to be got to in order to triumph. For example in Ashbourne in Derbyshire the goals were two mill wheels, several miles apart, and once the ball touched one of these wheels it was said to be "goaled". Again this curious convergence of football and sex: with the advent of goalposts a record of the score was kept by cutting notches on the posts. Whatever, the climactic event is this scoring of goals.

Goal scorers "notch" hat tricks, all adding to their season's "tally". This is the locus of the heightened emotion, of extraordinary ecstasy or the greatest despair. The "puke in the back of the mouth" moment as Joe Kinnear, the Tottenham and Eire full back, so eloquently put it on behalf of all defenders. All longing and dread hinges on such moments, which in our TV age are endlessly celebrated as "goal of the month" or "goal of the season". It is often felt—but I hasten to add not by me—that a goalless game, a no- score draw, equals a draw bore. That something is inherently less than if nobody actually scores. Just as for many (leaving aside Sting and the Tantric fuck masters) sex without orgasm seems to defeat the object. At one level—nothing prevents us saying at a conscious level—we want goals, the more the merrier, for our favoured team. It would be difficult to argue otherwise. Yet what psychoanalysis brings to the table, is that so often, unconsciously, we are after something else. And that might be described as a commitment to frustration, to disappointment. Which after all (and again it would be hard to entirely disregard) is indeed the lot of the majority of football followers.

Defences, and particularly the goalkeeper, are eager to "keep a clean sheet". This has nothing to do with some semen stained bedding. Nor is it a reference to some imaginary sheet hung up behind the goal prior to the advent of goal nets in 1890 (invented by James Brodie in Liverpool, as it happens) but stems from the Football League's requirement of an official score sheet. Forwards, in contrast, may suffer from a "barren spell". Teams may be plagued by a "goal drought", something "dries up". Whilst crowds, particularly those behind the goal, may play their part by "sucking the ball into the net". In other words the language underlines the notion of secretions, of juices, and when it all starts to flow "the floodgates open" and we may have a "goal feast"—soiled sheets and sexual fluids being the order of the day. And those most revered are the "star strikers", never "afraid to miss", invariably "gleeful", always "goal hungry", forever "goal grabbing" or in the case of the Leeds and England player Allan Clarke ceaselessly "sniffing". Perhaps to underscore the orgasmic connotation the term "finisher" crops up, not so much as a synonym for goal scorer, but descriptively or comparatively ("Romario is one of the best finishers in the world"). Out of the repertoire of the Blues singer Howlin' Wolf is a number called *Back Door Man* celebrating his sexual predilections. Goal "poachers" are often to be found at the "back door", otherwise known as the "far post". Such men "know where the back of the net is" for they all have "an eye for goal". In other words "they know the score".

But let us return to the examination of those reactions to the scoring of goals, which we cannot overemphasise, are so fundamental to the game. Desmond Morris has argued that it is mistaken to read the sexual into the embraces, the hugs and kisses, that the scorer will be engulfed by, now so commonplace. But let us remember that it was not all that long ago, certainly here in Britain, that such practices, usually associated with the "Latin" as in Mediterranean or South American temperament, were initially met with considerable disdain, scorn even. A form of "No sex please, we're British" possibly. Well, no, not according to Morris, for he seeks to emphasise their origins. Our initial, indeed founding experiences of hugs and kisses "is in the arms of our mothers when we are tiny babies". The Hungarian psychoanalyst Ferenczi went a considerable way to differentiate between the language of tenderness and the language of the erotic. And this is what Morris underlines: there can be non-sexual loving, expressed by the embrace as an expression of warmth and strong feelings for the other, particularly at intense emotional moments. The solidarity of arms round the shoulders at penalties after extra time, for example. And of course there has to be some truth to that. Nevertheless it is never so simple to completely disentangle the sexual. The French psychoanalyst Jean Laplanche did so much to underline the unconscious messages, the unconscious sexual messages, stemming from the mother that can so perplex the infant. "Enigmatic signifiers" is his term, congealing around a motif of a breast which is simultaneously a source of nourishment for the child and a site of the erotic for the mother. The breast as both providing and wanting.

In part the reductionism that psychoanalysis can so often be justifiably taken to task for congeals around Freud's emphasis on the insistence of our "instinctual life". Of returning everything to their sexual antecedents. In his *Five Lectures on Psycho-Analysis* Freud drew attention to "a far more expedient process of development called *sublimation*." Back we go to his idea that "the energy of infantile wishful (and essentially sexual) impulses" is not neurotically repressed or cut off. Rather this energy "remains ready for use . . . the unserviceable aim of the various impulses being replaced by one that is higher, and perhaps no longer sexual". So rather than actually fucking we opt to score goals or to gaze at others scoring goals. For according to Freud we "exchange the sexual aim for another one which is comparatively remote and socially valuable." Rooney at £27 million anyone?

It would seem that there has always been something para-doxical right at the heart of Freud's initiatives, as he found himself inaugurating something that he wasn't entirely sure that he was happy with. In other words there was something of psychoanalysis that appeared to be on the side of a disruption of convention, a dismantling of inhibitions, a removal of repression. By an emphasis on greater freedom, the psychoanalytic imperative suggests the possibility of satisfying forbidden desire, the possibility of transgression, the possibility of fucking in the streets. And murdering anyone who might get in our way. It can seem at times as if this is almost a psychoanalytic mission statement: the liberation of a suppressed sex life. At times Freud says as much. In his 1907 paper *Civilised Sexual Morality and Modern Nervousness* he wrote, "The injurious influence of civilisation is due to the harmful suppression of the sexual life of civilised people (or classes) through the 'civilised' sexual morality prevalent in them."

At other times it is almost as if he is addressing a FA coaching course. He wrote "In general I have not gained the impression that sexual abstinence helps to bring about energetic and self-reliant men of action . . . far more often it goes to produce well-behaved weaklings who later become lost in the great mass of people that tend to follow, unwillingly, the leads given by strong individuals." You can almost imagine George Best smirking in the back row.

But again things are never so simple. Our sexuality is for ever conflicted. Whether it is in the public domain where the talk is of the "battle of the sexes", or the private where as an effect of oedipal concerns our sexuality is conspicuously engaged in agonising struggle. Freud recognised that for us "the sexual instinct does not organically serve the purposes of reproduction at all, but has as its aim the gaining of particular kind of pleasure." And of course this recognition suffuses his ideas about our infantile sexuality, where all that matters is precisely this "gaining of particular kinds of pleasure". All akin to the pre-match warm up that inexorably, seamlessly spreads into the (adult erotic) game itself. Generating a particular kind of pleasure.

Football in all its sublimated glory operates as a paradigm of the polymorphously perverse, an exemplary alternative to contemporary anaesthetisations. Unfettered by hysterical considerations it can engage our desires unambiguously and directly. After all it is a "simple" game, and because of this, unlike actual sexual intercourse, will take up a place in most of our lives at a comparatively early age, for most whilst we are still in childhood. So it is both "innocent" and sexual, all at the same time.

Recently I was idly walking past a local primary school (lingering to gaze installs a curious self-consciousness in this day and age) where much of the cramped inner-city playground was taken up by a raucous game of . . . three guesses. What I was struck by was the quality of uninhibited frenzy, of intoxicating delirium that so characterised the kick-about. Embryonic Bellamys everywhere. To describe the scene as one of enthusiasm felt shallow: possession, wired, eyes shining, limbs pumping, hearts pounding, that was the order of the day. The yielding up of self. Tussles. Rucks. Those moments when the light drains from the eye. No appeals to an imaginary referee. Back and forth, occasional lulls. Inevitably the odd elbow in the windpipe, the pulling at a pullover, a raked shin, a theatrical collapse, all mimed from the subliminal archives of television. By and large without complaint. But above all emotion. Passion. Grazed knees, and above all else: the SHOUTING. A cacophony, a pandemonium of playground enjoyment.

Football operates as an umbilical tie to these uninhibited excitements but is framed by fantasy. Here it is crucial to recognise that fantasy is not simply reducible to a realisation of a particular desire in a hallucinatory way. It is not merely that we might at some level all wish to be animals in bed, thus potentially installing Norman "bite yer legs" Hunter as a role model. Rather fantasy structures our desire, almost to the point where it teaches us how to desire. This all turns around the idea that is so important to those of the Lacanian persuasion: the claim that "there is no sexual relation". There are occasions when such assertions as "la rapport sexuelle n'exist pas" (sexual rapport doesn't exist) can only provoke the inevitable rejoinder that "Well, you could have fooled me!" But much of what Lacan was trying to emphasise was that there is no *one* form of sexual relationship. In other words there is no universal formula which would guarantee a harmonious sexual relationship with one's partner. On account of this it is each to their own. We all have to invent a "private" formula or fantasy for our sex lives. One of Freud's most celebrated patients, the Wolf Man, had the following (rather analogous to one of the more infamous Allan Jones sculptures): where a view of the woman "from behind, on her hands and knees ... washing or cleaning something on the ground in front of her" automatically gave rise to love.

Although as Tina Turner might add *"What's love got to do with it?"*

And football is similar. Some of the fraternity find the need to walk round the ground in order to touch each corner flag in order to fulfil their desire. For others something of the experience is crucially missing if a programme is not procured. It is as if some memento of the occasion is a necessary ingredient, analogous to the underwear fetishist who builds up a collection of his conquests' clothing, all to bury his nose in at a later date. And you thought that you merely wanted to find out the teams!

But surely it is those teams, the players themselves (again we cannot fail to note the contemporary colloquialism for a so-called ladies man is "player") who are most intensely involved in the sublimated activity. The spectators, the fans, ultimately relegated to a more voyeuristic role. Perhaps more akin to the pornography addict, so desperately peering at the assorted images of women in simulated ecstasy, all seeking to satisfy that insistent itch, the doomed attempt to decipher the code: what do women want? But for the player, and how often is it said, "nothing beats playing", something more seems to be at stake. And that more is less. The sublimation here is where there is less consciousness of the body only for a more acute aliveness to emerge. As is always true in all our moments of unselfconscious performance. When we are utterly carried away, seduced by the delirium of the game, we forget ourselves in order to play. This delirious forgetting that so many of us longed for at school break-times, and the factory lunch hour, merely spawns the enhancement of memory, enchanted memories suffused with surprise, saturated with the excitement that only surprise can bring. The exquisite goal, the perfectly timed tackle, the sublime moment of ball control, all logged in the memory bank. So were Lacan to ask of football "Does this look like fucking?" at one level the answer has to be "No", but it certainly looks as if fucking has got *something* to do with it.

Losing: My Religion

For many of us in this secular age it is stating the obvious to acknowledge that religion, certainly in any organised sense, has lost its grip. We appear to have fallen out of love with it. As an effect of this there is an enormous vacuum, a God shaped hole in our lives. A situation vacant. And it looks as if football has become that which for so many fills that vacuum.

G.K.Chesterton, a devout Catholic, thought that when people stop believing in God it is not that they start to believe in nothing. Rather they'll believe in anything. Psychoanalysis, which can also operate as a substitute "religion", is unequivocally linked to love, although not necessarily love of the analyst. It is as if what is at stake is that psychoanalysis offers the potentiality to love with one's whole heart. Remember the religious rallying call "Love God with all your heart and all your soul and all your might.", and perhaps the same goes for football. Indeed it is hardly novel for football, both with the utmost seriousness and simultaneously facetiously, to be likened to a religious order. Its adherents seen as modern day equivalents of religious devotees, the away fans as hedge priests, all suffused with spiritual fanaticism, enthusiastically partaking in a secular communion.

Once again by an attentiveness to the language that is so often used we may glimpse some not so subliminal nuances. Frequently the pitch is referred to as "the sacred turf". Certain stadia or "temples" that the "faithful" flock to may be known as cathedrals. "La Catedral", as the San Mames in Bilbao is known, is one example; a book celebrating the history of Benfica's Estadio da Luz is subtitled "La Catedral" of Portuguese football. Sometimes teams are "sanctified" by name: St Johnstone and St Mirren in Scotland, St Pauli from Hamburg; by nickname: Southampton are "The Saints" (otherwise known as "southern softies" to some) or the obverse: "The Red Devils" whether it be Manchester United or the Belgian national side; or by the name of the ground: St Andrew's, St James' Park (be it Exeter City or Newcastle United). Directors' board rooms can be referred to as "the Holy of Holies". Manchester United's (or more properly Matt Busby's) compulsive quest for the forerunner to the Champions League: the European Cup, was known as "the Holy Grail", epitomised by the "Holy Trinity" of Best, Law and Charlton. Intriguingly George Best in recalling the 1968 European Cup Final had this to say, "I can still see Matt's face when he came on the pitch at the end as if it were yesterday. He wasn't crying, that came later, but he looked as if he should have had a halo over him, like the pictures you see of *saints*."

Supporters' bedrooms or garden sheds, stuffed with memorabilia, may be called "shrines". Star players or managers are "worshipped", the former sometimes spoken of adoringly as "young gods". Indeed at Easter 1999 the London Listings magazine *Time Out* featured on its cover "The Resurrection of David Beckham". He was dressed all in white, had a rosary round his neck, and his arms were stretched out in supplication. Inevitably this occasioned considerable consternation from various church leaders: "Unfortunate" was the description of the Church of England's director of communications, Dr Bill Beaver. The United Reform Church warned that "everybody has to be careful playing with symbols that are important to other people. These things shouldn't be walked over." Meanwhile Beckham has consistently displayed an uncomfortable sense of religious sensibility. Exemplified both by the Hindu inscription tattooed on his arm (albeit misspelt) and in that moment when he pronounced that he and "Posh" wanted to have Brooklyn "christened" but had not yet quite decided on "which religion". However, such deification is hardly restricted to Christianity for there is a golden statue of him in a vaguely squatting pose installed at the foot of the main Buddha in the Pariwas Temple in Bangkok, together with a hundred other minor deities. As yet no mention of Phil Neville in their midst.

But one player in Manchester United's history was indeed taken to be God, at least by fans decked out in replica shirts with the collar turned up à la Eric, with his magical number 7 on the back. The word "Dieu" or "Le God" printed above. Such religious connotations were strongly reinforced in 1996 when Cantona was "immortalised" in an oil painting. All this after his comeback from his kung-fu lunge at the Crystal Palace fan on that wintry night at Selhurst Park in the previous January. Interestingly this provoked his manager Alex Ferguson to find solace in heaven and hell metaphors. "Eric took us to heaven with that wonderful goal to beat Blackburn ... we were now taken to hell". The painting was done in Renaissance Italian-style, somewhat after Mantegna, by Michael Browne, a Mancunian artist. Resurrection complete having led United to a "Double Double", Cantona was depicted surrounded by his young acolytes such as David Beckham and Nicky Butt. (This time Phil Neville did make the line up, along with his brother.) The image combined Christian and Imperial Roman iconography, with Eric clutching a Cross of St George, somewhat akin to a risen Christ. Probably the sort of thing that would have made it into Tom Tyrell's book *Manchester United -The Religion*, had that not come out in 1969. But what most certainly would have been mentioned was the phrase "Phoenix

from the Ashes" so routinely used to describe United's magnificent reorganisation, their "rising again", following the Munich
air crash of 1958. On reaching the FA Cup final barely three
months after the disaster the phoenix, a pagan mythical creature
appropriated by Christian allegorists in the Middle Ages to
designate the Resurrection, was incorporated into the club badge.
It all becomes dangerously close to a tedious orthodoxy, but there
is more to come.

The term "icon", deriving from the Greek "eikon" or "image",
and informed with sacred connotations through the veneration
of Holy Icons in the form of painted images of Christ, the Virgin
Mary and assorted saints, is now applied to the more dominant luminaries emerging from the more prosaic confines of the
world of football. Again Beckham is a sullen instance of this,
variously described as a "sporting icon", a "cultural icon" (and
this is where he and Posh perk up) a "gay icon". Legend has
it that certain icons were depicted without human hands, as if
somehow invested with supernatural powers, leading to their
being hoisted aloft going into battle or lodged upon city walls to
repel furious invaders. Indeed certain players will be invested
with a particularly mythical status, hinging on their ability
miraculously to "turn" a game, to rescue a lost cause via super-
human efforts. In Naples murals of Diego Maradona, in spite of
or as an effect of his forty days in a cocaine wilderness, appear
as the modern day equivalent of those medieval city wall icons.
As an effect of such mythologizing it is not difficult to witness
fans bowing in "we are not worthy" obeisance. Sometimes daring
to touch the magical player, so analogous to the desire to kiss the
hem of a Holy Man's robe. A counterpoint to this will be the
"Judas" placards held forth in orchestrated demonstration by
outraged supplicants to greet the return of a former favourite,
whether it be Paul Ince at Upton Park or Sol Campbell at White
Hart Lane. All marinated in deep feelings of heresy and betrayal.
Something that, yet again, Arsène Wenger failed to see.

Superstitions such as Nick Hornby's sugar mice, not to mention the magical practices of goat sacrifices in Istanbul, or spell casting in the back of goal nets all over Africa, are commonplace as forms of summoning up the deities. And we have not even got to the hymn-like singing pouring forth from the terraces. Indeed some of the songs are actually borrowed from church hymn books, even if the crowds bellowing forth are hardly choirboy. Perhaps the most famous is *Cwm Rhondda*, the classic old Welsh hymn now better known as "We'll support you ever more", so frequently bastardised into "You're not singing any more". These are so often referred to as "terrace anthems", all an effect of numerous well worn religious tunes having been appropriated by clusters of fans, all up for a good sing-a-long. Anthems originally were sacred vocal compositions, often deriving from the Book of Psalms, usually performed by choral groups or large gatherings. Many of them are very old Black American Spirituals or Gospel songs, so emphatically linked to an expression of communal solidarity. Particular instances would be the anthem of the 1960s Civil Rights Movement in the United States *We shall not be moved*, for so long an Anfield favourite, or the rampaging "Glory, Glory Hallelujah, when the Spurs go marching on, on, on" of those magical European nights at White Hart Lane. Whilst the fans may not consciously make the connection many have their hands clasped together in search of divine inspiration, hoping that their "prayers" will be answered as their favoured ones so desperately seek to get something out of a crucial match. Perhaps particularly after a tiring "pilgrimage" to an away game.

Now there is nothing particularly original in this thesis, some writers being far more emphatic. The late Catalan writer Manuel Vazquez Montalban was particularly dogmatic that it is football that has become the only viable religion of the third millennium. His argument was that, following the end of the Cold War and the dissipation of the grand narratives, all aided and abetted by the crises within Western religions, there is this spiritual void to be filled. And football fits the bill. "It's a post-modern globalised religion, in that it is perfectly in tune with the commercial needs of mankind, intrinsically linked to business and consumerism. It's cathedrals are stadiums, it's gods footballers, it's faithful the millions of fans who not only participate in this ritual every matchday, *but practice their faith on a daily basis, thinking about and reflecting on the deeds of their gods.*" It is not so much that men think about sex once every ten minutes but rather it is football that is constantly on their minds. A frightening thought.

Nevertheless it may be important to recall that in the past the church service did not only operate as a place of communal prayer. Simultaneously it operated as an assertion of group identity. All that hymn singing provoking a sense of belonging, of inclusion. Now it is the football match, divorced form any theological underpinnings, which will encourage a fierce display of local and indeed international allegiance. In so many ways similar to a religious gathering the match brings together large crowds, more or less bound together by a common and strongly held belief. Or is it that there is "safety in numbers", for is what binds people together a collective disbelief, an assumption, an anxiety that "we are going to get gubbed again"? All congeals around the team, although to claim that the fan truly "believes" in their anointed XI may be going a step too far, however much there will be the unstaunchable mantra of "Keep the faith". Psychoanalysis always wishing to say that such an incantation only draws attention to the anxiety that this "faith" is only too easily slipping away. And out of the Cup.

But just how deep may we genuinely go with all this? A mere game, the cause that binds together being no more than the success of a particular side, standing in the place of the seemingly loftier concerns of a political or spiritual nature. Shallow seems its proper level, which is not to say that it is not interestingly shallow, importantly shallow even. It may be utterly crucial to pay considerable attention to the entirely superficial if we are going to approach any understanding of the contemporary world. Yet in form and practice there are certain similarities linking football and the sacred. Quite possibly in the primitive, archaic rituals of this "sacred" playing, and playing the game of watching football, we may find what is indispensable for any community's well being. Put another way we may find there its spiritual well-being, that which makes life for both community and the individuals within it worth living. Again for many this might seem crass to appear to equate the boorish aggressivity, the beer monster, the junk-food chomping, the pit-bull sensibilities of the stadium with, for example, the exquisite nuances of Vedic sacrificial lore and the wisdom of the Upanishads. But let us turn to Plato and his ideas with regard to play. After all he appeared as a toga wearing midfield player in the Monty Python football team, somewhat prone to tugging his beard as the game swirled around him. Play, and why should football be any different, he understood to be crucially "outside and above the necessities and seriousness of everyday life". Whilst his conception of religion was that it was "play consecrated to the Deity, the highest goal of man's endeavours", thus allowing a potential, even an essential link between the two. In other words a fundamental structure that enables a gradual extension of the notations of mere football, of mere play, into and onto the consciousness of the Holy embodied in these higher creeds. If you believe in such things.

Psychoanalysis or psychoanalysts so often can have a compulsive tendency to head off in the direction of somewhat self-defeating abstraction. But they would be far from having a monopoly on such matters. Indeed, Montalban can be accused of forcing the metaphor, irrespective of whether it really stands up to closer inspection. For example, he describes the more physical, more structured, ultimately more cautious football of England, Germany and other northern European countries as inherently right-wing whilst the more creative and intuitive Latin football as intrinsically leftist and progressive; more on the side of the angels, closer to God. As an immediate counter-argument there is the thought that the stolid team-ethic of the Scandinavians parallels their social-democratic political backdrop, whilst there is something fascistic in the more narcissistic star (leader) worship so characteristic of the Italian, Spanish and Argentinian football cultures. Lazio in Rome was Mussolini's team (still supported by openly fascist Ultras with the execrable Sinisa Mihajlovic for so long their pin-up boy) whilst Real Madrid could call on Franco's support. But as they say the devil so often has the best tunes. Or teams.

A potentially more interesting thesis is one regarding that one unstinting pocket of resistance—a good old fashioned psycho-analytic term—by the United States in its reluctance to embrace "the beautiful game". Whether it brings anyone closer to God or not. For this I am indebted to the Lacanian analyst, Richard Klein, a founder member of the English Lacanian grouping CFAR. Now on the whole Lacanians tend to be somewhat resistant themselves when it comes to America, in particular to "American psychoanalysis". In this they follow their master, for Lacan was especially virulent in his critiquing of what he saw as a "delinquent" conception of Freudian psychoanalysis stemming from American initiatives. Rather than focus on an individual's adaptation to prevailing societal norms, a form of fitting in, a doctrine centred on the conscious ego, which Lacan saw as the "American" way, he wanted to place emphasis on a search for the truth of the subject. This would involve the gradual unveiling of the unconscious desire that will always be found within the illusions of the ego. Inevitably this might run utterly counter to any ideas of fitting in at all. Quite simply he thought that "American psychoanalysis" had lost the plot. Freud was none too keen himself, "I don't hate America" he wrote, "I regret it!"

But back to football. Klein points to an "American" culture of impatience. The demand for the immediate, whether it be their food, as in fast, or their forms of play which so often are characterised by a principle of "stop-start", whether it be American Football or the "three strikes and you are out" of baseball. For them the more European sensibilities of the "dialectic", the prolonged struggle involving a "back and forth", is like a joke that they just do not get. One only has to look at the North American Soccer League and their incapability to accept the idea of a drawn game: for them it had to be back to the "stop-start" of the utterly wearisome "shoot-out". In the culture of immediacy there has to be a winner. Sadly the FIFA president Sepp Blatter is of a similar persuasion, claiming to SID, a German sports news agency, that he would be advocating the "abolition of the draw". Such sensibilities ignore the occasions when a draw is a highly satisfactory outcome for one or other of the teams, and sometimes both. In May 2004 Tottenham came from 2–0 down to hold Arsenal 2–2 with the aid of a last minute penalty. Nothing would have been served by deciding a winner through further penalties for Arsenal had the point that they needed to clinch the Premiership, and Spurs were only too delighted to have wiped the contemptuous smile from their opponents' faces. No English fan will forget David Beckham's famous free-kick which enabled England to force a 2–2 draw with Greece up at Old Trafford and gain automatic qualification for the 2002 World Cup. In other words draws are all part of the draw. For an incomparably more far reaching analysis of such resistances, particularly those concerning the US, *Offside-Soccer and American Exceptionalism* by Andrei Markovitz and Steven Hellerman comes highly recommended. But whatever way you look at it America remains a last bastion of "non believers".

What may be worthy of further reflection is the simple fact that this linking of football and religion as an idea both refuses to go away and may possibly reveal something important about the very nature of the game. Without recourse to Plato. Perhaps the utterly crucial point is that few other professions carry with them such uncertainty. By and large you do not find plumbers crossing themselves when confronted by a particularly maddening blocked sink. Nor for that matter psychoanalysts in the face of the intractable patient. Which is not to say that there is so much certainty saturating the situation within the analytic consulting room. But I digress, for unlike footballers, plumbers and psychoanalysts more or less hold their destiny in their own hands when it comes to their job. If a pipe needs fixing, either it gets done or it does not, depending on the ability of the plumber, and will be judged accordingly. People are not like pipes but you get the gist of it.

However, from an early age footballers learn that no matter how well they may perform individually, the result can never be guaranteed. During one week in the spring of 2004 three of the overwhelming favourites in the Champions League: Arsenal, Real Madrid and AC Milan, were all knocked out of the quarter-finals. More prosaically that season in England in an FA Cup Fourth Round replay Tottenham were leading Manchester City—down to 10 men, 3–0 at half time. Home and free you might think. Nevertheless they contrived to lose 4–3 in the last minute of the game. Sides from Manchester more recently seem to procure divine inspiration in finding themselves 3–0 down at half time at White Hart Lane, Manchester United running out 5–3 winners in September 2001. All this simply shows that uncertainty—part of its enduring charm after all—is one of football's invariants. In part this is because it is a team game and partly because there are a multiplicity of factors which can never be entirely controlled, such as refereeing decisions, injuries to key players, the elusive entity called "form", and of course the ever present "Lady Luck". The fan simultaneously will face the same unknowns, these same intangible and intractable factors. All with the added problem of having even less (and consequently more frustrated) impact on the outcome. One thing is for sure: uncertainty and the unknown will inevitably give rise to the metaphysical, whether it takes the form of religion or Jimmy Melia's lucky underpants.

Given this unrelenting backdrop it is hardly surprising that faith, whether it be genuinely "religious" or more talismanic— such as the compulsive making the sign of the cross on entering the field of play—is so prevalent in the game. Faith by definition is that which goes beyond the straightforwardly rational. It is a leap from the strictly logical to a belief in the incredible, and is utilised to explain what defies or cannot be explained by reason. And it is all over the place. Lurking under shirts we find scrawled on the pristine T-shirt variations of "I belong to Jesus", and we are not just talking the Pentacostal Taribo West, the former Inter Milan and Derby County stalwart here. The Deportivo La Coruna manager, Javier Irureta, is renowned for a veritable catalogue of tics and superstitions. He insists on wearing the same coat to the game, rain or shine; he refuses to sit down until his side has scored, and chews the same bit of gum from kick-off until the post-match interview. But crucially he made a forty mile pilgrimage on foot to the cathedral at Santiago de Compostela as a form of thanksgiving for the extraordinary, the "miraculous" come-back by his side against the former European Cup holders, AC Milan.

Almost as if there is something embarrassing about it, as if it makes us feel a bit anxious, there is a tendency to distance the game from such overt religious connections. When football and religious practice come together in the media it is usually in one of two ways. Either the religious elders, coming on a bit like the last guest at a party that has already begun to disperse, rail splenetically against football's encroachment on both cultural practices and contemporary values. The Archbishop of Canterbury, Rowan Williams, cites that TV series *Footballers' Wives* as emblematic of our culture's incorrigible selfishness, all too louche and loutish. Meanwhile Pope John Paul II, allegedly a big Liverpool fan, wants his Sundays back. "When Sunday loses its fundamental meaning and becomes subordinate to a concept of 'weekend' dominated by such things as football" he said, "people stay locked within a horizon so narrow that they can no longer see the heavens." Probably such sermonising would not have had too many converts amongst the Millwall faithful, for "heaven" (otherwise known as the Millenium Stadium in Cardiff) was where they all felt they were heading having overcome Sunderland in an FA Cup Semi Final in 2004. With a guaranteed European awayday to boot.

Alternatively we are subject to the "weird and wacky" newspaper diary piece, ranging from dragging up the former Coventry City youth keeper David Icke, always good for a sneer, to Carlos Roa, the Argentinian goalkeeper in St Etienne when, following the Beckham sending off, England went out of the 1998 World Cup. He retired to the Pampas to await the Apocalypse due at the end of 1999, slipping back into the Argentine Premiership once the millennium had passed off without incident. In the next World Cup in 2002 the Italian coach, Giovanni Trapattoni, was to be seen at press conferences clutching a small vial of holy water "to ward off negativity", presumably a reference to the Italian press corps, dissatisfaction guaranteed for all eternity. Hardly surprisingly the Vatican could barely contain itself, criticising Trappattoni for "turning religion into pagan superstition".

But perhaps there is a tendency in all cultures to turn to the mystical, whether religious or otherwise, as a way of defending against the sheer contingency of our being. And football is no different. It suffuses its discourse: Stanley Matthews was the "Wizard of the Dribble", Roberto Baggio the "Divine Ponytail", and possibly the greatest of them all Diego Maradona will be forever associated with "the Hand of God" incident in the Aztec Stadium in the 1986 Mexico World Cup. Intriguing to speculate as to quite why his Buenos Aires streetwise shrugging off of the persistent TV interviewers immediately after the game has struck such a chord. Hardly because anyone took it to be literally God who leapt and punched the ball past a bewildered Peter Shilton in the England goal that muggy afternoon in Mexico City. Nor that anyone, despite his sublime displays throughout the tournament, took Maradona to be God. But perhaps some genuinely believe that it was God that allowed Maradona to cheat and get away with it.

Both chief Rabbi Jonathon Sacks and a former Archbishop of Canterbury George Carey support Arsenal. They first bumped into each other in 1993 when Manchester United won a fixture 6–2, following which someone impertinently suggested to Rabbi Sacks that the result must go someway towards refuting the existence of God. His response went "What it proves is that God exists, it is just that he supports United". Precisely what countless away fans have always believed when yet another "nailed on" penalty claim goes begging up at Old Trafford. Or when Pedro Mendes' shot unequivocally crossed the line.

An Italian journalist, Giampaolo Mattei, recently came out with a book which was made up of a collection of one hundred testimonies from footballers—including the likes of Ronaldo and Batistuta—all concerning their relationship to religion. Mattei's argument is that football's overbearing importance is unequivocally linked to filling that spiritual void, particularly for the supporters who transfer a need to believe from religion and/ or ideology onto football. But it is not just the supporters. Simultaneously footballers, in turn aware of an increasing form of unspecified pressure linked to the idolisation involved in this assertion of a pagan faith, revert to the refuge of religion. Back to those T-shirts and the compulsive crossing oneself. Some such as Rowan Williams appear to wish "if only" that were true, rather than the more popularised recourse of the players to place their bets on compulsive hedonism.

Hull's most famous poet Philip Larkin has described all churches as having something of the "ornate and mad" about them. Sheffield Wednesday's ground at Hillsborough and the Olympic Stadium in Stockholm—part castle, part mansion, part cloister, all circled by flag poles—are merely a couple from a vast repertoire of football grounds across the world that amply fulfil such requirements. Rather like the Belgium artist Panamerenko, who would fill gallery spaces with enormous caricatures of transportation, all so redolent of the potentialities of flight but which were actually forever grounded, football grounds (as with churches) often resemble vast, expired ships or spacecraft which have run aground in our urban midst. Anyone who has visited that graveyard of ocean going liners on the mudflats north of Chittagong in Bangladesh will be struck by the similarity to sports stadia. Both seemingly beached, glowering and simultaneously glowing, subliminally throbbing. More usually in the past, just as with churches, the stadia would be situated in an inner city location. Although increasingly the prevailing trend, as with the mental institution (note the emergence of the notion of asylum, of sanctuary) is for them to be set up in out of town green field sites. Some, such as the Reebok Stadium in Bolton (particularly when floodlit), the Stade de France in Paris, the San Siro in Milan, Puebla in Mexico all have that almost transcendental quality as if they are about to take off, speeding through the air when actually they are going nowhere, utterly rooted to their community. Of course football grounds come in all shapes and sizes, and many will be more pre-war tug boat than the aforementioned ocean going liners.

Another game, another writer. The magnificent C.L.R James in his book *Beyond a Boundary* knew only too well the significance of such sites. He was considering the meaning of the famous cricket club Shannon, who operated on the savannah, the huge expanse of green in Port of Spain. "Shannon" wrote James, "had more than mere skill. They played as though they knew that their club represented the great mass of black people on the island. As clearly as if it was written across the sky, their play said:

Here on the cricket field if nowhere else, all men are equal, and we are the best men on the island."

Visiting a stadium when it is empty, so much like peering into a church, is to be met with the huge reverberant silence, informed by ancient air as if the passion and the possession, those oohs and aahs still dimly resonate. All feeding off a wintry light, whatever the season. Holy ground, sacred turf, but places of what? Churches are traditionally providing comfort and sanctuary, shelter from the storm. And whilst it can be argued that football ceaselessly offers sanctuary from the ravages of sexual politics, and there is always the emphasis on "home advantage", comfort is hardly what is sustainable when it comes to a football stadium. In so many cases there will be implicit memorials to anguish, to blood rites. So often gaunt, grey and unwelcoming, heavy with resonances of unrequited sacrifice. Always the ultimate sacred act. Etched with grimaced effort and unstinting exertion, stadia can be faintly yet insistently menacing, underwritten by notions of the "fortress". At some level—as with churches—this is part of their charm, but at the same time all quite mad.

Possibly all that religion has provided for the world is unceasing hatred, magnificent music, and overwhelming architecture. Leaving aside the music, pretty much what you would find at an "Old Firm" derby up in Glasgow. For the most part churches, mosques and synagogues, as with stadia, are simultaneously places of awe and dazzlement. Floodlights will always intensify the colour, "the celestial light" angling down from the phallic protuberances. Desmond Morris in his *Soccer Tribe* designated floodlights or at least the floodlight pylon as "huge tribal totem poles". Sometimes these take the form of gracefully tapering concrete pillars but more usually are open metalwork towers propping up clusters of powerful lamps. Rising high above the surrounding landscape, invariably visible from afar, so invaluable as "homing" guides for the itinerant supporter, they operate as a constant reminder of the "hallowed" ground that lies beneath them. Any lover of football grounds will automatically, when passing through any town either by train or in a car, compulsively strain to catch a glimpse.

The lights amplify the luminous green that is so emblematic of the "field of play", colloquially known as "the park". As with psychoanalysis where there is an emphasis on "the couch", in football what matters is what happens "out on the park". Note the importance of the green. During the Nazi occupation of Prague the only green spaces allowed to those wearing the Jewish star were the city cemeteries. Green and its link to consecrated space, to life, became a constricted arena at once so redolent of the immanence of death. But this is how Geoffrey Green (ah, how that word insists), that doyen of football writers, described the first Football League match to be played under lights, in February 1956: Portsmouth v Newcastle at Fratton Park, ". . . there arose a vision of the future. In twenty, even ten years time, will all football be played under the stars and the moon? There is much to recommend it. There is a dramatic, theatrical quality about it. The pace of the game seems accentuated, flowering patterns of approach play take on sharper, more colourful outlines. In the background of the night the dark, surrounding crowd, half shadow yet flesh and blood, can produce the effect of a thousand fire-flies as cigarette lights spurt forth."

And always that noise, oh that noise, that unmistakeable roar, the thousand throats in communal unison. And unmistakeable it is, as any addict will know. On holiday many years ago I was walking with my family through some woods in Northern Poland. And then that sound, nearby. An immediate exchange of knowing glances, a rapid agreement to meet up in the little café where we had lunched, and I am speeding through those woods and in through the gates. Heaven. All courtesy of the assembled congregations of Wisla Krackov and Gydnia FC.

A stadium, like a church, has the potential for exerting a fatalistic fascination, an insistent attraction for any culture's morbidity. Unwaveringlly drawn by the metallic click of the turnstile to that towering eminence on the hill, for within its fastness is the place for ritual worship: not so much God the particular footballer, as football itself. Football as spectacle. All this is informed by an in-mixing of fear and the magical, but ultimately framed by the oppressive reassurance of defeat. Just as all churches have a large Christ covered with His bleeding wounds, evoking a mystical glow, so all stadia will have remnants of the wounds of defeat etched into the fabric of the place. Melancholy is never far away, as it is difficult to entirely purify, wash away the trace elements of agony of suffering, so essential to all genuine play or love. As the Balkan love song has it "The one who has not known suffering has not known love". For it will be true for any side, however successful it may have been or is now, that some aspects of its history will be informed by seasons of the eternally joyless, of pouting, suffocating lethargy, of morose resignation. Once again the close season dreams are consigned to feed off ancient glories. At Poissy, a gloomy suburb at the end of the RER line out of Paris, in the frites and merguez cabin tucked away behind the main stand it is possible to glimpse a sacramental fragment: a stiff card programme propped up on a shelf commemorating a French Cup tie against the comparative "giants" of Strasbourg from some distant season. And you can find such consecrated items the world over, lodged in the crevices, the crannies of stadia. Talismanic residues that sustain a faltering belief.

A generalisation it must be acknowledged, but by and large it is men who like maps. They do not seem to do very much for women, Amy Johnson notwithstanding. Sometimes women appear to have almost an aversion to them. But a familiarity with inner city maps will remind one that two sites are invariably marked : churches and sports grounds. Simon Inglis of *Football*

Grounds fame, described by the Irish Times as "the spiritual leader for us poor souls who suffer a sinful quickening of the pulse when we see floodlights looming" (spiritual leader, souls, sin?) drew attention to how architectural books are always full of descriptions of even the dullest of churches. Yet Nicholas Pevsner in his guides to *The Buildings of England* barely touches on football grounds. Wembley and Hillsborough are allowed merely a passing mention. Yet in every community there they are. Incidentally Inglis was later to record in his book *Stadium Odyssey* how he trawled through Buenos Aires, where apparently there are more football stadia than public libraries, visiting as many as he could manage in a week. He did this accompanied by none other than a mate who it turned out was a psychoanalyst. It was only later, back home but still savouring the delights of that city, "the world's finest ciudad de los estadios", that his wife pointed out that, of course, he had been in therapy throughout that week. Naturally enough, in good humour, he demurred, "What me? Mariano happens to have been a psycho-analyst. But that didn't mean anything . . . Why would I need therapy? The idea was absurd. I just write about stadiums." At least he makes a living out of it. For so many of the rest of us, the obsession just insists.

But if there is this link between football and religion, both in the sense that football as community uses religion and in the sense that football stands in the place of religion in so many communities, what would psychoanalysis have to say about it? About the use that religion has for us? Freud, possibly at his most reductionist, came to the conclusion that "reduces religion to a neurosis of humanity". He sought to explain "its enormous power in the same way as a neurotic compulsion in (our) individual patients". All as an incorrigible enslavement. Perhaps it is a good thing that he never sunk his teeth into football.

Never less than dogmatic he claims that he "never doubted that religious phenomena are *only* [my emphasis] to be understood on the pattern of the individual neurotic symptom . . . as the return of . . . important events in the primeval history of the human family". Religion is pathologised, read off in terms of "symptoms". Utterly illusory, religion is a form of clinging to mummy's apron strings. A petulant refusal to leave the warmth and comfort of the parental house, cocooned in the fantasy of the Omnipotent Being keeping loving watch over all men. At other points he will quite explicitly associate "the dogmas of religion" as bearing "the character of psychotic symptoms, but which, as group phenomenon, escape the curse of isolation". Bring in Larkin and that theme of the white coats. Religion, and by association, football offers sanctuary for those of us under the sign of the deranged and the demented. Perhaps we are on the right track after all.

Freud, as has become common knowledge, had this thing about the "Oedipus complex" which he took to be "the nucleus of all our neuroses . . . so far as our present knowledge goes." So it will hardly come as a surprise that his understanding of religion congeals around this foundational complex, all being reduced to "one single concrete point . . . man's relation to his father". It is as if Freud wanted religion to do two things. One was how we all might go about dealing with the unbearable uncertainty of things and our intolerable helplessness in the face of this. As if a belief in God would facilitate a manner of controlling the world around us. Or at least allow the idea that there was someone or something in control. The idea having a close proximity to an ideal: the single great primal Father, a directing deity, imbued with all power and authority whether it is Allah, Buddha, Yahweh, or Alex Ferguson. The origin of which is ancestor worship (bring on Sir Matt Busby). So long as there was an investment in this recognition of a "supreme being" then one would have some form of share in this greatness. The narcissistic dividend being enhanced self-exaltation, possibly leading to an incorrigible sense of smug superiority so charac-teristic of United fans. The sort of phenomenon of "my daddy's bigger than yours" that led to the formation of the "Anyone but United", the ABU club here in England. The "Anybody but Bayern" being the German equivalent, envy always being more tolerable within the safety of numbers. But these ideas of the ideal would be taken up by vast swathes of people, would be preserved by them as a precious possession, which in turn would enable them to maintain a pride in being "a chosen people". "The Galacticos" of Real Madrid are but one example, but the same principle operates for the loyal supporters who clamber on the team bus to watch Billericay away. All suffused in unerring assumptions of reward, of distinction and ultimately—in Tokyo—world domination. Or back in Billericay a Charity Cup Final on Canvey Island.

Simultaneously via recourse to various sacred texts, bodies of instruction as it were, we would all be enabled to reassert some mastery over our "internal world". We can retrieve some control over our potentially disastrously uncontainable spirited selves. The "beast" within. It would enable us to appear to hand over, to transfer our one time imaginary omnipotence to God or the Gods, whilst simultaneously surreptitiously never truly abandoning it. And all this would run parallel to or correspond with what is going on with our actual parents, or parental substitutes. In other words there ought to be a rule about it. A set of commandments. Otherwise known as *The Laws of Association Football* (at least as far as the microcosm of football is concerned). All this has to be "believed" in, and without such belief it feels as if the whole thing would catastrophically fall apart. As if football would go completely "Kenny Burns". Allowing that many may not be familiar with the Nottingham Forest and Scottish defender, a word of explanation (perhaps Craig Bellamy would be a contemporary instance): something of the deranged. Coming straight at you. Gnawed fingernails. Mean and hungry. Yelling, furious, wanton, wired, forever on the edge of terminal loss of control. The diabolical red mist merchant. Wonderful anarchy.

For this is where the second aspect of religious belief or practice comes into view. It is an attempt to slough off a sense of original sin or guilt. Freud's idea being that this sense of guilt has been with us for thousands of years, "and has remained operative in generations which can have no knowledge of that action". This "action" or act paradoxically is not so much any actual act in itself but the intensely powerful effect of phantasies of particular actions. Phantasies, and the "ph" denote that these are unconscious fantasies, which we are not as yet aware of, of killing and devouring the father, of returning the maternal body to us, just us. For Freud our guilt lies precisely in such murderously rebellious feelings against an authority, divine or otherwise. For the Jewish philosopher Emmanuel Levinas, who cast such a shadow over late Twentieth century philosophy, we all live with a burden of guilt precisely because of our infinite and incalculable responsibility. We all have an ability to respond to "the otherness of the other", indeed are called upon to do so. This other can never be fully "captured" through social categories or designative names, but always a certain response will be owed. And this burden is inescapable. And yet escape is unrelentingly sought after. And here we may note that football is endlessly referred to as escapism, or as *The Observer*'s Will Buckley would have it, an escapism from which we cannot escape.

And so, via Freud, we may come to glimpse why the Christian story of Christ, the ultimate redeemer, who via the Crucifixion took on the guilt of the world in order to relieve others of theirs, has such immense popularity. As if all we have to do is to believe in God and it's all sorted. So is that what is happening on a vast scale from the Bundesliga to the Japanese J League? Thousands of lost souls by paying homage to something that stands in the place of a deity, are all engaged in an unconscious search for redemption, all seeking some albeit momentary release from the pressure of unbearable unconscious guilt. Is that what this escapism is about? Nothing to do with "her indoors" after all?

Take this as a hypothetical example: on a Saturday afternoon four thousand penitents pitch up at Gigg Lane in Bury of all places. All taking up their position as members of the terrace chorus. All are part of the primeval brotherhood. All suffer that burden of infinite responsibility. But via the suffering of the appointed hero, namely the team, that band of anti-heroes, all are in line to gain redemption. Writing in *Totem and Taboo* Freud said "In Greek tragedy the special subject matter of the performance was the suffering of the divine goat, Dionysus, and the lamentations of the goats who were his followers and who identified himself with him . . . the tragic hero became, though it might be against his will, the redeemer of the Chorus". Sean Goater anyone? In the Middle Ages all this revolved round "the Passion of Christ". But in our day and age "the special subject matter of the performance" all centres on the passion of the Gigg Lane faithful and the fate of their leading goal scorer. Or at least as an illustration of the point.

Freud went on to elaborate on our emotional ambivalence, the simultaneous love and hate towards the same "object". For him he saw this as lying "at the root of many important cultural institutions". Always the origin was understood to stem from "the father complex", and this enormous overvaluation of the father. Not difficult to see this foundational ambivalence enacted or displaced onto the figure of authority—the brandisher of the red card, the Law, otherwise known as the long suffering referee. So needed (the bloke who ran *the Times* side in the Fleet Street mid-week League was occasionally reduced to brandishing a £20 note outside South London DHSS offices on a Tuesday morning in order to procure one) and simultaneously so resented.

What Freud wanted to exemplify was the part that religion played in enabling a shift from a patriarchal horde, seething with destructive impulses towards foundational authority figures, towards a more fraternal, civilised (if discontented) community. And it is a moot point when hooligan excesses abound whether football entirely succeeds in facilitating just such a shift. Which is not to say that it has nothing to do with such considerations, whether knowingly or not.

For many the first name that come to mind when one thinks of psychology, and most certainly psychoanalysis, will be that of Freud. But it is likely to be followed, almost immediately, by the name Jung. One of the difficulties of philosophical or psychoanalytical systems which purport to reveal the constitution of the world is that they can so easily lend themselves to being no more than the involuntary confessions of the psychological peculiarities of the author. Put another way merely their neuroses writ large. And just as there is a complete absence of anything to suggest that Freud had any interest in football at all, simultaneously it is difficult to entirely dismiss the sense that, when it came to religion, there was something about it that he just didn't get. It is not that there is a lack of coherence nor an intelligence to his considerable thinking on the subject. But nevertheless something seems to be missing. As if he is too clever by half.

Psychoanalysis can so often fall into the trap of failing to acknowledge that what is going on is always invariably singular, that it is not representative of anything at all, and can never be encompassed within a totalising conceptual system. Jung, with his signature concepts of "archetypes" and "the Collective Unconscious", of course can be enmeshed in similar difficulties. However he sought to differentiate himself from Freud. At times he seemed quite desperate to unshackle himself from any devotion to the worshipping of the sexual that he so associated with Freud. Spirituality was much more his thing. Although one might add (needless to say really) he was sexually involved with a number of his patients.

He wanted to emphasise dreaming as a form of religious experience. It is in our dreams that we may encounter the spontaneous up-welling of religious symbols. Often these will be unknown to the dreamer, but all going to show that the unconscious had a "naturally religious function". Obviously there is an inherent undecidability in this, a circularity of argument even. Jungians tend to see the symbols in any dream as potentially religious whilst Freudians can cast it all as sexual. Ever eager to return religion to its more traditional spiritual significance Jung nevertheless brought a more pragmatic underpinning to things. For him if religious experiences, and now we insert football experiences, help to make life healthier, more beautiful, more complete and satisfactory to yourself and those you love, you may safely say "This was the grace of God". Quite how safe that is to assume rather begs the question.

Rather than stain it with trace elements of neurosis, however much that may be the prevailing condition, Jung wanted to insist that religion was an antidote to the "pathologies of modernity". There is a grumpy, irritated tone to much of this, as if it all stems from the fiftysomething school of "things-ain't-what-they-used-to-be". We are all going to hell in a handcart. Perhaps that is why his followers so often seem to come from the brown rice and sandals brigade, with Prince Charles muttering at the daffodils bringing up the rear. The principle grumble was that we have all lost our connection to "instinct" and the natural. It is via religion that "the childhood soul of mankind" was preserved in "numerous living vestiges." Possibly rather foregrounding some of Freud's concerns.

But undeterred, Jung was consistent in his concern regarding this apparent breakdown of traditions. For him "instincts" were understood as "the most conservative element in man". Conservative now having a plus sign attached. In as much as we have allowed ourselves to be uprooted from such considerations we are lost. Instincts now seem to be assumed to operate as a static set of rules, as if we all really know, or at the very least ought to know, what is good for us. Something similar seems to come into play whenever Prince Charles begins to hold forth on the subject of architecture. Not that we can hold that against Jung.

Modern man is over-identified with his conscious knowledge of himself, and the city dweller is most of all estranged from the natural. "What a rabbit or a cow is, one only knows from ... the dictionary or the movies" was Jung's claim. Heaven knows what he would have made of the contemporary football ground and its obsessions, its partly puerile preoccupations. Not to mention a disused aircraft hanger beyond the M25 throbbing to drum 'n' bass, all pumping on E-highs. Back to nature, bare chested drum- beating in woods seemed more his sort of thing.

But could there be something that football brings to the table, despite being for Jungian sensibilities, at so many levels, a locus of alienation? After all Jung was hardly blind to the multiplicity of ways in which religion with its codified systems, represented in the dogmatism lurking in so many religious statements, was caught up in a leading us astray. Yet he put his faith in religion. Maybe football with its faith in fun allows some other form of knowledge. In Jungian terms perhaps football will enable us to be in touch with the Collective Unconscious, however briefly. In his *Psychology of the Unconscious Processes* he proposed that within us all, as well as a whole inventory of personal reminiscences, there lay the "great primordial images". These he saw as the most ancient and universal thoughts of humanity. And they are as much feelings as thoughts, all linked to fundamental laws and basic principles, and in as much as we are cut off from these we place ourselves at the greatest risk. The risk of being condemned to everlasting despair. Perhaps all those estranged city people are unwittingly resuming an engagement with the natural, the "instinctive", when they lace up their boots. Rubbing on the embrocation so analogous to the heady intoxications of incense suffusing the Catholic Church, and filing out onto yet another scruffy recreation ground. All to return to the exquisite joy of mud on the knees, thus preserving "the childhood soul of mankind", back in tune with "Mother Earth". All restoring the link with these primordial immutables.

That's as maybe, but we might note something of all this moving in the direction of the previously mentioned Albert Camus and his claim that "All that I know most surely about morality and the obligations of man, I owe to football."

Maybe there is method in the madness after all.

Football is Therapy

Psychoanalytic listening is potentially something special, something other. But it is never pure, for of course there is tiredness, there is being afraid, there is being elsewhere. Nevertheless there is something in Lacan's assertion that there is no practice, activity—his word is "praxis", call it what we will, that is more real in the sense of trying to touch the heart of experience. And football has that capacity: to touch our hearts. But neither psychoanalysis nor football is ever all there is, nor can they take the place of a whole host of other aspects of our lives. But both the intimacies of the consulting room and the vast expanse of the tumultuous crowd, not to mention the breathless physicality of throwing oneself into a game, allow a focusing on the experience of how people might be together. Allow an exploration of these feelings—so saturated in the desire to produce meaning, to get a result—on and on, further and further, at times beyond all reachable meaning, to move beyond into the registers of seduction. Freud called such explorations "free association". Football is officially termed "Association Football". Both, in their separate ways, entangled in the wildness of these possibilities, these potentialities of associating freely, whether it is between two people, amidst the team, or as a member of the crowd. The only occasion that I can recall being kissed on the lips by another man (allow for my sheltered life) was at the 1988 European Nations semi final in Hamburg when Holland went 1–0 up against their most hated opponents: the host nation. A big ginger bearded bear of a man, in Hell's Angels leathers, covered in orange badges, tasting of spliff.

Lacan was always keen to emphasise something of the quality of the flow, the movement specific to unconscious process. He would use terms such as "cut" and "pulsate". He would describe unconscious process as "pulsations of the slit", a rhythm of opening and closing, the visible and invisible co-joined, all with associative links to the dark continent of the feminine. And football has a potential for a similar rhythm. An opening and a closing. A constant pulsation. Entangled in this is the issue of penetration. We as patient, analysand (as ever a problem of terms) are penetrated, ruptured, taken over, taken in by the pulsations of the game. As is the analyst. Freud had this famous maxim "Wo es war, soll Ich weden": where id was, ego will be.

Lacan put it otherwise, "I will go where it is. I will go where you are, follow you, go with you-it. I will return to the place of dreams, to the place where dreams come from, through the dream naval . . ." The football fan "will go where it is", it being the site of assumed enjoyment. Up to Villa Park say, or, as the song puts it "over land and sea, and Leicester". Forever dreaming. This might be thought of as a form of coming home (*"Football's coming home"* so decorating Euro '96). In psychoanalysis the home is the field of the unconscious, the unrealisable, the irrepresentable. And we have not even begun to examine the vexed question of whether it is all "structured like a language". But whether it be psychoanalysis or football something of a similar order prevails. "Keep the faith"—faith that by returning over and over again to feelings of haunting dismay, of intense frustration (albeit interspersed with moments of exquisite, glorious gratification, of sublime and rowdy triumphalism); faith that by returning to this hour after hour, week in week out, we find ourselves feeling more real, more alive. Why else would people spend years in analysis or spend a lifetime devoted to their team? Each week is a testimony to this dedication. To the cause. All supporting our aliveness.

In a world (or at least a Eurocentric, mid-Atlantic world) so dominated by a psychoanalytic thinking it might not come as a surprise to allow the thought that everyone is in therapy. Of course they are not literally, any more than everyone is into football. But is football the form of therapy that most people are in? Do both psychoanalysis and football share the characteristics of a phenomenon where the centre is everywhere, whilst the circumference is nowhere to be seen? Lacan described the position of the analyst as "the one supposed to know", the assumption of this potentiality for knowledge occasioning love. In football we all know that our team is "the one supposed to win", and of course we all love our team. But it is a frustrated love. Freud had his famous maxim that "therapy takes place through deprivation" and sometimes it looks as if both football and psychoanalysis fall prey to becoming an exercise in disillusionment.

But it is not for knowledge that anyone will enter a psychoanalysis, not really. Rather it is a particular experience and we may note that there are continual convergences between the experience of analysis, therapy, whatever we might call it, and so much of the experiences so enmeshed in football. It is not difficult to recognise that both football and psychoanalysis are instances of self elected trauma. Both involve an identificatory and emotional tie, which psychoanalysts refer to as transference, and one could say that all football fans have precisely that with regard to their chosen team. Fans are always distinct from spectators, as exemplified by a fifteen year old boy talking to his father as they stumbled dispiritedly out of Brisbane Road after their side, Carlisle United, had been relegated from the Football

League, "You know Dad, at Arsenal we were just spectators. But here we are fans." That difference can be called transference.

In whatever way we approach these two quite different sites of involvement there will be a converging set of recurring and invariable traits. There is always something of a trance state, a form of possession that was spoken of before as a "trance-itional space", something wedged between ordinary wakefulness and being asleep. And this gives rise to a host of competing narratives. The popular song from the early 1960s *Football Crazy* warned of the "terrible football team" that will lure one into the pathological degeneracy. At the same time psychoanalysis can be seen as arousing a dire dependency from which there will be no exit. Possession is so often taken to be on the side of illness. On the side of the damned. Part of its charm. Traditionally it is understood as a violence that is perpetrated by malignant spirits, the intrusion of a pathogenic agent. And so many are possessed by football, possession so frequently conflated with obsession. Somehow football is always "other" in that it is always other than representation. Of course there are innumerable videos of games which can be endlessly replayed but its essence, utterly convergent in playing and/or watching, right at its heart, its fun, is always already elusive. What is on offer is an altered state, and so, like psychoanalysis, is taken to be extraordinary. In some sense it is transgressive in that it moves, as does all play, beyond reason. Yet simultaneously it is banal, it is so very ordinary, so everyday, or thanks to Sky TV, so every-night-of-the-week.

The thing about football is that it takes you out of yourself. In a curious way it allows one not to be "oneself". In other words it is a "self" cure. We cannot do it by ourselves but we do it for ourselves. So much of this is via the furnishing of a group with a particular language through which unexpressed or inexpressible psychic states will have their place. At one level meaningless; certainly in the wider scheme of things it really does not matter if, for example, Wrexham win away at Swansea City;

yet simultaneously operating as an integrative or (spell-) binding principle. As was so very true of the early treatment of hysteria by Breuer and Freud, when a considerable amount hinged on the so-called "ill" being symbolically (which is another way of saying socially) recognised by the group. And we all engage in the glow of mutual recognition. We are all "Tottenham" in the Antwerp Arms.

Paradoxically possession is not so much on the side of a loss of identity but is now utterly reversed. It is a sign, a form of kissing the badge, a call to arms, a finding one's place. A coming home.

But home, like homes in general, is not always comfortable. At times it may be an unsettling thought to recognise how much we are forced to share our familiar space with ghosts, residues from some other time. It is stating the obvious to say that this idea of home is a far from simple one, any more than it is a simple place to be. This complexity is caught in a word that Freud had a fondness for: *unheimlich*, which translates into English as "uncanny". What is *unheimlich* is simultaneously both homely and unhomely, familiar and yet strangely strange. To describe the stadium or the dressing room, any more than the analytic consulting room, in such terms touches on this strange familiarity because, like the people with whom we share them, they are known to us both intimately and not at all. Home is the place where we are both most and least ourselves. We might ask what precisely are we referring to when we invoke this notion of "home"? After all it may not be where we live—more often it is where our mother lives. Is football, like India, "mother"? Home is so often linked to identity, both personal and group, yet the experience will always be cross-fertilised by the two. Is that what football brings to the table? This possibility of simultaneously both finding and losing oneself, swept up in the intoxicating flow of "home" advantage?

But of course it is not just any old game that will work, which is not to say that football is the only game, despite the claims of the *Sunday Times* sports editor who said that the three most significant sports for his readers were "football, football, and football", or Delia Smith who said "Football and cookery are the two most important subjects in the country". Although, judging by the plethora of TV programmes on the subject (doing them up, buying one abroad, how to move up the property ladder) our home has become more recently an insistent concern. But I digress. The games that can facilitate this "therapeutic" aspect are those that both stage and implicitly acknowledge the risk element in a ritualised indistinction between self and other. In all probability this is a rather pompous way of saying that they will be team games, although we must be especially cautious if we were to think of the analyst and the one who comes for analysis as "a team". The "cure" operates via the utilisation of a particularly heightened, elevated element.

In the case of football it is the team that is in the place of the analyst. This moves in the direction of a confused or fusional state, allowing an escape from the more habitual social or "symbolic system". I observe two England fans in a bar in Istanbul, the night before England play their crucial European Nations qualifier. One asks the other "Who are you?" The answer, "I'm Villa". Is this why football is so repeatedly referred to as "escapism", although to establish quite what the escape is from is more elusive, and where does this escape lead us?

Where both football and psychoanalysis converge is this critical therapeutic ingredient of trance. Which is another term for rapture, for possession. Crucially this is linked to a dramatisation of this undecidability between the possessed person and that which possesses us. As the psychoanalytic critic Mikkel Borg Jacobsen said our identity is a passion and our passions are always identificatory. In my identification, my passionate identification with my team, we are as one. The trance or light hypnotic state induced by that team (or analyst) is continuous with the possession suffered by the supporter (the patient, the analysand). But what exactly is this trance state a remedy for? In what sense is it therapeutic? What does it mean to describe it as a self-cure?

Perhaps it frees us from the incorrigible alienation of our selves, so enmeshed in the passion for representation. The crucial thing about football, its essential character if you will, is that it is an experience that is *lived* outside of representation. And what did Bion, a celebrated British analyst, say of the analytic tie? "It is ineffable (irrepresentable)" And what is our malady? What is it that we all suffer from, if not our pathetic selves? Our passion for identity.

One of the ways of understanding the statement that "it is a man's world", other than a plea to officialdom that football is a contact sport, is that there is an emphasis on the specular. In other words something that can be erect(ed), gazed upon, wondered at, or put another way: represented, is what is valued. At times it is as if anything that is outside the "closure of representation" does not count, does not exist. And what we unceasingly engage in, leaving the Tantric hermit on the Himalayan hillside out of this, is a compulsive erection of an image of ourselves. Despite the insistence of the mantra that "anything we take ourselves to be, we are not", or Lacan's emphasis on the *meconnaisance* (misrecognition) involved in all such egoist representations it is so difficult to avoid. Clearly what counts for many is football as spectacle, as event, as game, as occasion. Some like to get there early "to soak up the atmosphere". The whiff of something "other". An occasion for possession. In as much as the trance is linked to remedy it is linked to the imitative. A woman who was coming for analysis, described taking her son to football for the first time. She mentioned how she had noticed that initially he kept his little fists somewhat self-consciously tightly clamped inside his coat pockets. Until that is, he could contain himself no longer. He too was carried away, seduced, en-tranced, gesticu-lating, pointing, waving, all modelled on the "mad horde". Speech no longer that of a subject, but rather an inspired speech, a chanting, an exhortation, a raging, in which self became merged, indistinguishable from another.

The Church has never shied away from notions of possession, allowing that it can be both diabolical and simultaneously a potentially mystical union with God. However there has always been fundamental dualism lurking in Christian thought in that there has been a clear demarcation between Good and Evil. In similar ways, in as much as we think within similar dichot-omies, our culture has consistently attempted to marginalise the disturbed and disturbing. Always seeking to extrude, to culture out, dump outside of the city limits, outside the social body. Any notion of asylum is always secondary to the primary desire for exclusion. Note the horror that will inevitably unfold if there is any suggestion that a football club relocate or a therapeutic community pitch up at the end of the street: Oh No, those back-yard anxieties come to the fore. Uncontainable, unmanageable fear and loathing.

Pinel, the famous liberator of psychiatry, wrote of "religious madness" and "melancholia via devotion", sounding pretty much like the lot of most football fans, indelibly lodging possession under the sign of "illness". Unquestionably propelled by hooligan ecstasies that continue to plague the football world, possession seems fated never to be purified entirely from the persecutory and demoniacal. Nevertheless, rather like a small therapeutic pocket lurking amidst the grim back wards of the large mental institution (David Cooper's innovative "Villa 21" up at Shenley comes to mind), healing potential sits amongst the chaos. And that healing is via the way of hypnosis, otherwise known as "affective rapport", or in psychoanalysis "transference analysis". Freud worked very hard to differentiate himself from his master Charcot, seeking to dissociate from any suggestion that psychoanalysis was tainted with vestiges of magnetism or hypnosis. He was particularly dismissive of any notion that what was going on was this weasel word suggestion. Yet what else is going on? Somebody says something to me, it suggests something, I respond, it suggests—can there ever be any exit? And despite his conflicts with the Hungarian analyst Ferenczi—almost in spite of himself—he actually integrated trance, possession, in mild and manageable doses into the psychoanalytic project. For after all psychoanalysis is merely a chapter in the history of trance.

But Freud knew something was up, something of the homeopathic principle of treating like with like, for he coined the troubled term "transference neurosis". The solution had become the problem. The dependency installed by the psychoanalytic involvement needed to be unravelled, to be analysed. The spell needed to be gently broken. Of course one of the delights of "going to the game" or peering round the pub is gazing at others trance-fixed. Spellbound by identificatory love. Reassuring glances. One is not alone. Safety in numbers. Infinite belonging.

Within the confines of the psychoanalytic treatment there is the well-known phenomenon called "negative transference". It is another way of saying that the person coming for the analysis does not like the analyst very much. But so often on closer inspection what is revealed is that it is the analyst who is stuck, caught in an ambivalence about the trance that psychoanalysis has provoked. The idea that resistance is always on the side of the analyst becomes irresistible. And it is not the analyst who has "hypnotised" the person who comes for analysis, rather it is psychoanalysis itself that provides the possibility for that person to become hypnotised—by none other than themselves. Now psychoanalysis—and it can be thought that its very identity is at stake in this—wants to insist that it is the *analysis* of the transference that is the place of the healing, the therapeutic moment. But what if that was necessary but not sufficient? Or furthermore what if the truth is that, rather than any sophisticated analysis of this transferential state, supposedly leading to some "resolution" at the end of the treatment—what more often emerges is drift? That the whole thing is allowed to drift. Indeed some would passionately argue that the extent to which this transference is referred to, is analysed, is that which will lead in the opposite direction. It will have the inevitable and irredeemable effect of binding the other more and more interminably within the analytic tie.

As far as football is concerned drift is the operative principle. "Negative transference" towards one's team or towards the game itself is expressed by a drifting away. Can't be arsed to go training, no longer going to the game, less compulsive reading of the match reports, increasingly vague attentiveness to the results. Meaning fades.

But wherever a particular analyst may situate themselves in relation to this, whatever "school" they may support, with all the attendant spasms of spite and malice that can so disfigure football rivalries, it is possible to argue that all the great hypnotic-magnetic therapies are modelled on the illness itself. All propose to artificially induce an aspect of the difficulty spontaneously within the trance state, and this is a line running from Mesmer (football forever mesmerises), Puysegur, Breuer and on via Freud, Klein and Lacan. Perhaps we all "feel better" after an afternoon or evening session at the football, allowing the trance state itself to work its magic, irrespective of the result. Well actually no. Possibly that is where football and psychoanalysis irretrievably divide. In football to get a result is everything: whole communities are manifestly affected by the winning or losing of crucial games, as factory productivity levels will bear witness. But perhaps "feeling better" was never the aim of the psychoanalytic game, more being on the side of "feeling alive". Football and psychoanalysis converge once more.

Nevertheless there is something of immense importance—after all it so addictive—which is entangled in this pulsation of possession and dispossession. This incorrigible flow of forgetting oneself. The altered state of letting go of oneself, when one's own "proper" identity, so linked to propriety, flies out of the window. Everybody now in favour of possession by another identity, some other self, which is none other than oneself. And all of this, even better, is seen as perfectly normal both in the consulting room and in the stadium. Or can be. For whether it be the primitive tribe and its shamanistic rituals, psychoanalysis and its emphasis on "the unconscious", or football and what it has the capacity to induce, the message can be distilled as essentially similar: "Truly you are no longer yourself, but that's just fine, so be yourself, that is another". And via an acknowledgment of these "other" or unconscious aspects of oneself, a more integrated self can emerge. That is the theory. Or as Baudrillard would have it, surrender to that fundamental dynamic of our being: seduction. Allow oneself to be carried away. To be lead astray. The call of contagion. Savour the madness.

Implicit in this is an acknowledgment that language and the social order are not all there is to human experience, and football—which can be reduced to being "childish", "stupid", "empty of sense", "incoherent"—simultaneously anchors that realisation through repetition and ritualisation.

Clearly this thinking has never left the confines of Winnicott's initiatives regarding transitional space, or to use a more technical term, transitional objects. Just for a moment let us concentrate on the ball itself. That foot-ball, that relationship between a part of us, our body and something other, in this instance a ball. What counts, what inaugurates it all, is not the ball as such, but our relationship to it. Like thumb sucking. What Winnicott has to say about mothering is never simply reducible to a dual relationship, precisely because of these transitional inputs that operate as a third term. The transitional object, the teddy bear let us say, enables us to move from one state, an imaginary idealised state of fantasised omnipotence to something more realistic. Or let us imagine that in Diego Maradona's case in that little shack in Villa Foirito, an impoverished neighbourhood on the periphery of Buenos Aires, it was a little football. Take it away from the end of his foot and he is inconsolable. Consigned to the anaesthetisations of cocaine sex nights from here on in.

Crucially this object can survive the most intense love and hatred. A father taking his four year old son to a game for the first time was considerably taken aback when his little boy asked, in a mixture of awe and anxiety, "Why is everyone so angry?" Immense frustration, that's why. Souness in spades. Frustration with the game itself, that defies mastery, frustration with the team, always beyond our control, frustration with a particular player, frustration at not being that particular player, at not being any player at all. For most of us, there was not even that Brando moment in the back of the cab in *On the Waterfront*. No talent, no hopers. Strictly amateur. Peter Hillel, my co-conspirator in the Tottenham caper, my season ticket companion of so many years, always found defeat a particularly bitter pill. Invariably we had barely got out of the back of the ground and into Park Lane before he exploded into the predictable spittle flecked cocktail of frenzy and fury, "That's it, I can't bear it, I'M NOT COMING AGAIN!"

And something similar is commonplace in consulting rooms across North London (and Leicester) only for the person concerned to arrive promptly for the next appointment. Freud was always very clear about it; frustration is what makes us ill. Wilhelm Reich took this very concretely, setting up the school of thought that claimed "an orgasm a day keeps the doctor away". But a life without some frustration is inconceivable, although the notion of a charmed life perhaps holds out for this imaginary impossibility. For the psychoanalyst this idea of frustration turns around the potential disparity between what I feel myself to be, my ego, and what I want to be, my ego ideal. Too big a disparity, frustration overload. This want-to-be may involve a fantasy of complete mastery of the analyst, never losing control for a precious minute. A woman that comes to see me confides that she finds it unbearable if I blow my nose, if I cough. In that moment she is abandoned. In football the wish could be for absolute control of the ball, or of our favourites winning every game. But there can only ever be that inevitable rendezvous with what Lacan dubbed our lack-of-being, that never ending struggle against loss. Psychoanalysts have this term "working through". This is the idea of returning over and over again to some particularly conflicted area of one's being. That somehow the more unmanageable aspects of us, principally those frustrations, will not so much be resolved as "lived through". As children we are called upon to bear our frustrations, but perhaps it is crucial that as adults we do not succumb too easily, whilst never entirely letting go of the recognition that some things are simply unobtainable. One season there was considerable derision when the Arsenal manager Arsène Wenger mused on the possibility of going a whole season without losing a game. That year it seemed premature, presumptuous, and frustratingly for him and his club it did not work out. But unbowed by such disappointments he merely returned the next time around, freshened up his side and with a surging vigour Arsenal went through the league season undefeated. Hats off indeed. Something about not taking "no" for an answer.

Whilst leaving Arsenal's European disappointments to one side (and who is to say that they, those disappointments, are not in the process of being similarly addressed as I write this book?) such bolstering of omnipotent fantasies is distinctly rare. For most, player or fan, torment is the more usual. Indeed the relief and respite, those brief, ecstatic moments of bliss are in part a function of their rarity. Torment merely being deferred, placed in abeyance. Of course we long for that bliss to be everlasting, we are co joined with the paranoid and their longing that one could be in "complete control", to live a life without ever being disconcerted, to never drop a point. Which is to miss the point entirely. The previously mentioned imaginary sign (cribbed from "Throbbing Gristle") over the door to my consulting room begins to take on another meaning: as if it is only through the guarantee of disappointment, of allowing precisely that, that one can be assured of other possibilities coming into being. Even for Rochdale.

Conclusion

Psychoanalysis is to be, if nothing else, a fundamental re-description of human nature. A description of what it is that we value and how we go about pursuing our goals, with its unerring emphasis on what we shy away from, on what we are not as yet aware of, on that which we seek to sustain as unspeakable. Yet there always seems to be the problem of quite what to do with that which people are entirely conscious of. It is as if at times psychoanalysis in its rush to unearth the hidden, the subtle, the forbidden, fails to see the wood for the trees.

So with this in mind, I would like to conclude with a story from a young woman, one of the people who at that time was coming to see me for analysis, and it concerns where we began: that Freud Museum (and the University of East London) conference on "Football Passions". It so happened that in her kitchen she had tacked up a poster, a flyer advertising the event. One of her brothers was visiting and over a cup of tea it caught his eye. He had a more than passing interest in football, being an enthusiastic Sunday League player in South East London (we shall leave aside his interests in his sister's interests). He got up to examine the poster more carefully.

It seemed to arouse a certain belligerence, and jabbing a finger at it he said, "What is this bollocks?!" Turning to his sister, with a trace of contempt, he continued, "It's not very difficult, is it?" She, faintly alarmed but simultaneously amused, replied, "What isn't? What's not difficult?", "The answer to the question 'Why is football so popular?'", came the response. A slight pause, mild bewilderment from the sister, and then he said, with considerable emphasis, "It's because it's a bloody good game, that's why!"

Quite.

Inevitably there is so much that I have not said, so much that I have held back in relation to my love affair, its intensities and its lamentable disappointments, its offer of eternal disillusionment. I am thinking of the smoke-filled, overheated football specials slowly and frustratingly returning from the Midlands after another Tottenham exploit, pulling into Euston in the middle of the night . . . the mugging, the stabbing—thankfully neither serious nor painful—but undeniably shocking, on the way to the FNB stadium for the opening game of the African Nations Cup in Soweto . . . of the scissor kick goal I scored up at Mansfield in an AFA Senior Cup tie (after all I didn't get so many). I am thinking of finding myself, having got off the airport bus in Belfast, gazing into a mild heat haze with the city set before me, and how I experienced this sudden surge of happiness, for no particular reason, except that I was alive and off to football in a strange and unexplored ground, so aptly called "The Solitude". For that precious moment free, free of myself, seduced, carried away, and that was a moment of singular preciousness precisely because it would not come again, or at least not precisely in that way. Of hotel rooms on the Paraguay and Brazilian border swapping stories and generally talking shit long into the night during the 1999 Copa America—this is a form of paying homage to one of the finest football writers of them all, Hugh McIlvanney.

One morning during the 1986 World Cup I found myself sitting opposite him on a press bus heading off to the Estadio Olimpico in Mexico City. An old mucker of his clambered on board, and smiling towards Hugh, asked "What did you get up to last night?"

"Ah, the usual . . . a few glasses and talking shit" came the languid response. Of course. Tequila and Bull anyone?

Of how much back at the Copa, we—Alex with his plethora of inside stories about Alex Ferguson, Martin who runs a programme stall at Charing Cross station on a Saturday, and Southampton Steve, with his dreams of flying football fans all over the globe, laughed and laughed. Of the quiet football intelligence of the former professional cyclist who Peter and I sat next to in the Lower East Stand at Tottenham for so many seasons. Of the headline in the local paper screaming "Shrink has problems of his own", a few days after I was sent off up at Barnet. Of the delights of witnessing what David Miller of the *Daily Telegraph*, with over forty years experience of covering international football, described as one of the finest games that he had ever seen: a 0–0 draw between host nation Mali and Nigeria in the African Nations Cup, only to be followed by a hectic scramble out of the 65,000 rammed into the National stadium into the Bamako night to find Salif Keita doing his thing in a cramped suburban club. But this is only to scratch the surface of the memories of the madness.

But a few words as to how I got into it all, or more pertinently how it got into me. Football not being a game so much, more a virus, a contagion. I recall one moment idly lying in the bath a number of years ago when the thought came to me that I could give it all up. I could simply decide to have nothing more to do with football. I could walk away from it without a backward glance. It has to be said that it was a fleeting moment. Very fleeting. Some—such as the philosopher Jean-Paul Sartre and his

Parisian coffee bar cronies—might dub this an existential moment. A moment of sublime freedom, when just for that instant I could glimpse the possibility of "noughting the past". I was free to choose. I was free to go. But simultaneously it was utterly illusory, for it was no more possible for me to "give up" football than to give up eating. Quite simply I have no desire to. It's all too enjoyable.

But do I have any sense of the origins of this addiction, this obsessive entanglement? From an early age I think that I had concerns as to what constituted "manliness", in part an effect of having, at least from my perception, a somewhat distant and disaffected father. In his late thirties he was diagnosed as suffering from the degenerative condition, disseminated sclerosis. And although he worked very hard to keep its ravages at bay somehow there was always the hovering spectre of his ending up in a wheelchair. After I had driven myself into the dust on the 1967 Hippie trail to Kathmandu I found myself utterly incapable of running. I was only twenty-three. This lasted for about three months, and principally was as a result of an in-mixing of sustained drug ingestion and chronic malnutrition. I had managed to contract a comparatively rare tropical disease—tropical sprue—which involves the corrosion of the stomach lining, as a consequence of which little nourishment was percolating through; I was down to about seven stone.

It was then that I was acutely conscious of a long-running, but long suppressed anxiety that, as an effect of hereditary factors, I would end up like my father. Running being the operative word. It was as if I never stopped running, running away from that anxiety and running into the arms of football. At university in Dublin I had played football almost every weekday afternoon in College Park, desperately struggling to get into the First XI. And once I was out of the Tropical Diseases Hospital following those debilitating months wandering across the Great Sand Desert of Iran on my way to the Himalayas (taking in Afghanistan v a

Russian Under 23 XI in *that* stadium in Kabul on the way) I was immediately back in the fray: out on the park on a Saturday afternoon, Sundays, mid-week mornings. I couldn't stop. Like quality racehorses, good players are always full of it: running. And I was running after that. Big time.

Mick Channon, the England and Southampton footballer, said that it is not that one gives up playing, rather it gives you up. Mine was an utterly undistinguished playing trajectory by way of Woodford Town reserves, the Happy Wanderers Charity XI (made up of assorted ex-professional footballers including the legendary original cheeky chappie, the old Fulham favourite Tosh Chamberlain; the disc jockey David Hamilton; the odd Python; a whole host of less celebrated TV stars, and even less celebrated "ringers" such as myself), Woolworths from the London Commercial League—known as Pointers FC (why? because people came from all points . . . oh dear. Although curiously almost everybody bar me came from about a mile radius of the Star pub off the North End Road in Fulham), *The Times* of the Fleet Street Mid-week League and on to playing for Hampstead Heathens Veterans at Corinthian Casuals Football Club one Sunday in February at the age of forty-eight. My wife Haya said that it was always going to be a painful business when I had to stop. Excruciating actually. Anterior cruciate ligament snapped in two. But something of all this is captured by an old Fleet Street Mid-week League contemporary, Phil Shaw, who covered Scotland for *the Independent* for many years. Playing for the Scottish Press contingent he was substituted with the call "Off you come—you've suffered enough."

I notice that hospitals crop up twice in this narrative, with their inevitable associations with sickness, with pathology. Yet it is not that I have spent so much time in them, although I began my psychoanalytic apprenticeship out at Claybury Hospital in Woodford Green. It had been the result of a suggestion by Adam Limentani when I had gone along to the Institute of

Psycho-Analysis at the age of twenty-three to find out how I might go about joining the mad horde. The upshot was the suggestion that what I needed was some experience of being around the psychologically disturbing. Yet I think that is what had always drawn me to football—in the nicest possible way.

It was as if the disturbed, the deranged and the delinquent were where the action was. The hard boys. Where the sex was. And where would you find them? Scattered about the playing fields and clustered behind the goal, that's where. For the anthropologically minded can I suggest Aldershot's Recreation Ground and its covered end as offering a particularly virulent instance of this thesis. And of course there is something homosexual about it all. Why else would one spend so much time watching, passionately watching, men run around in those shorts? Why else would one want to be one of those men oneself?

There is a theory that we are born into language. We are surrounded by words long before we acquire our own. In other words our subjectivity is informed by what we are subject to: the plethora of conscious and unconscious messages that will lead us off in certain directions. And yet there was not much conversation about football in our household. Or at least not until my brother and I got going. Not much? Not any. As far as I know neither of my parents ever went to a football match, and if they did they certainly never mentioned it. My arrival in my prep school football team seemed to pass without notice. But there was another locus of possibility five minutes down the road in the shape of my father's father: my grandfather. He had been the local grammar school headmaster, and would vaguely promise to take me to a game but never did. Although he did introduce me to the delights of Test cricket up at Lords when I was twelve.

However on occasions he would tell stories about matches that he had been to at St James' Park in Newcastle. Stories of grimy, coal black miners coming out of the Durham coalfields, pouring onto the terraces, all swearing and shouting . . . from the off—

raucous, rampaging delight. Unable to get out of the heaving mass to relieve themselves, a cock would be unceremoniously produced and streams of steaming piss would slowly seep down through the crowd. I was hooked by what to an impressionable boy seemed incontestable images of the real thing: real men, phallic men. Loud, virile, and above all else, up for it. Football men. And somehow I wanted in on it. I wanted to be a hot spur.

It was around this time that I began to drench all my food in vinegar, a subliminal identification with imaginary *men*, real men that I had spotted doing something similar in local greasy spoons. Working mens' caffs. Of course this was a reaction to, a rejection of my own father. A rejection that felt mutual. Locally he was known as "the boffin". He was either closeted in his study fiddling about with fossils, or had disappeared up to the Natural History Museum in South Kensington. Probably fiddling about with other women, whilst exposing Piltdown skulduggery. For some time there had been a sense of a non-specific breakdown in relations between him and my mother, but all this was veiled by a spurious concern with appearances, not least because of anxiety with regard to his parents just down the lane. No doubt football offered itself up as escape. Escape to freedom from any concerns about all this, as I smothered myself in mud yet again, or sought refuge in the newspaper scanning the results.

Don't get me wrong. My recollection of my childhood is one of pretty much unstinting delight, but looking back, all sustained by considerable dissociation. And right at the heart of this is a fantasy. A fantasy or a dream of non-castrated phallic energy, sustained by a raw and roaring vitality. And it all stems from the *grand*-father.

Yet it is none other than my father who may have played, probably unwittingly, a crucial and possibly defining moment in the unfolding of the addiction. Other that is to the part that he played in driving me in the direction of the reaction formation, the negative identification with none other than him. Negative operating rather akin to the photographic negative, sustaining a latency. One autumnal evening when I was eleven he came in from the commuter special, out from Baker Street through Betjeman's Metro-land to where we were living: Amersham-on-the-Hill. The end of the line in more senses than one. And he had a present for me. Archived away in the memory bank it stands out, principally because it felt so unusual. Unusual in that I was getting a present from him other than at Christmas and birthdays. Not because of any particular meanness on his part, but because it felt like a momentary rupture in his seeming indifference to me. But also because of the present itself. In all probability he had picked it up from the WHSmiths on the station platform. It was the Football Association Year Book for that season, 1955–56, and of course I still have it. Many, many years later it was to come in useful in assisting Mike Collett with his research for *The Guinness Record of the FA Cup* which appeared in 1993. But mainly it stood out because it was *just what I wanted*. A sign of love. And curiously rather like those "transitional objects" that Winnicott made such play of, there is something of an undecidability that I continue to cling to. Was this little annual a response from my father to an already established interest on my part or was it a critical, a founding moment, sending me off in a particular direction? By that age I was certainly aware of football—not merely the playing of it at school—but also the whereabouts of the results in the newspaper (with the fate of Tottenham Hotspur already being of particular concern). But like so many of my preoccupations I had assumed that this was utterly private, when in all probability it was singularly transparent. But certainly I am pretty sure that football, although having its place, had yet to take up the place of centrality that it now does. Important. But not as yet one of the loves of my life. One of the symptoms.

But I sense that what is at stake in this is a refusal, a concerted effort on my part to fend off any acknowledgment that my father had any feelings for me. This has two benefits: firstly by placing him in the position of the offender, the indifferent one, I can justify my indifference towards him. Secondly this is an indifference that I seek to sustain as it protects me from acknowledging that I have feelings towards him, with all the attendant anguish that would provoke. I glimpsed something of this as an effect of a conversation with one of the people who comes to see me for analysis. What this conversation drew to my attention was something I had conveniently suppressed: television.

It is quite possible to sustain the theory that we are now in the third stage of the evolution of modern football. In the initial stage, approximately from 1870–1885, football was something principally that was played. Then for the following hundred years or so football became a spectator sport, something that people watched live, at grounds. But now for the most part the bulk of live football that most fans enjoy is "football on TV". In pubs. This was hardly the situation in the early 1950s. Even by the early 1960s it took considerable "homework" to track down where it might be possible to watch the Cup Final in Dublin—no shortage of bars, but one with a TV? Indeed there was no TV in our household until 1959, but just down the road at my grandparents there was a small set. Black and white of course, perched on a little table in an upstairs room. And it was only ever watched on "special" occasions: the Coronation and . . . Cup Finals. The first one that I can recall was "the Matthews Final" in the Coronation Year of 1953. I have vague recollections of increasing restlessness after about 70 minutes with Bolton 3–1 up, preferring to drift out into the garden to kick a ball about, only to be subject to excited, agitated even, calls from my grandfather . . . and to breathlessly arrive back in the little room just in time to see the magical Sir Stanley ghost past all opposition, cut the ball back for Perry to rifle home the last minute winner. Another year, another game: this time Len Shackleton, the "Crown Prince of Soccer", tearing apart the then World Champions West Germany, at Wembley in the autumn of 1954. To the best of my recall my father was never present on these occasions. Or if he was it was only for a cameo appearance poking his head round the door, feigning a form of benign bewilderment, as if it was all a little beneath him. Something that, periodically, I would reprise when my family was enjoying *Dallas* or *EastEnders*. Yet looking back, it would have been inconceivable that he did not have some sense, however vague, of the shared excitement going on in that little upstairs room.

As far as I can recall there was no other gift, nor any further mention, that would in any shape or form lead me to feel that he had noticed anything in relation to my absorption in football. Certainly no parental presence on the school touchline. Not that consciously I would have welcomed that, for a central element in all this was escape. It was as if that small annual operated as a message, a hint that I was only too ready to take, a nudge in the direction of "Go on, my son, go where you have to go". Football offering refuge from the emotional disaster zone that my parents relationship had become. Divorce just did not seem to happen in the 1950s, or at least not at my school amongst my contemporaries.

But inevitably in part this absorption in football must have been done with one eye on my mother. No doubt wanting to be in the place where her desire fell, I allow that subliminally I assumed that knowledge did it for her. After all, what else do "boffins" have going for them? And football simultaneously offered a knowledge from which my father was excluded; in other words it was some *other*, rivalrous knowledge. Around about the age of twelve I remember contemptuously chiding my father for "not knowing who the World's most valuable footballer was" (answer: John Charles). All this going on right under my mother's nose. Later it was through perusing the books at her bedside that the seeds of my interest in psychoanalysis were sown. It was as if I had discovered what knowledge in particular turned her on— she took Winnicott to bed with her.

A little later in one of his books from one of her shelves I was to come across what to me was the extraordinary idea that guilt *precedes* the crime. This idea so vividly struck me as offering something far more intriguing than the intellectually unsatisfying sociological explanations that I later found to be peddled at the Institute of Criminology at Cambridge. But simultaneously didn't I just want to get into the place of her desire? To displace my father. Which lead to this interest in guilt in the first place.

The first match that I ever went to was with my school. The first eleven were taken up to a game at Wembley, an England International against Yugoslavia, on a dank, dark Wednesday afternoon one November. It was 1956. Maybe the light had something to do with it, a particular Metropolitan glow that continues to unfalteringly provoke excitement. But something happened that afternoon that seems to have set the tone for my spectating habits from then on. Encouraged something even, and it turns round the issue of knowledge and its conspicuous exhibitionistic display.

I was enormously enthralled to be sitting behind the goal, to actually be at the game . . . at last. In goal for England that afternoon was the Tottenham keeper of the time, one Ted Ditchburn. I had noticed an odd mark down the side of his fairly voluminous shorts, and after a while I turned to my assembled schoolmates and authoritatively announced, "See that thing on Ditchburn's shorts? That's his lucky rabbit's foot." Within seconds a somewhat bony finger lightly jabbed my shoulder, and I turned to see one of those ubiquitous figures from 1950s, globule precariously dangling from an equally bony nose, cloth cap shading ravenous if now somewhat amused eyes,

"That's not a rabbit's foot son, it's a smear of pitch marking." he announced authoritatively, and quite loudly. Cue considerable barely suppressed snorting and sniggering from the entire prep school party, and a faint reddening of my face.

I know that I enjoy telling this story. I also know that, as I said, far from discouraging me it has almost propelled me into more and more loud-mouthed assertions from a multiplicity of vantage points in stadia around the world—a right "gobby gob-shite" forever anticipating the jab to the shoulder. The sense is that somewhere in this tale is a crucial element of the structure of the fantasy. A question, a psychoanalytic question, would always be where or how is the fantasizing subject inscribed within the fantasmatic narrative? For it is far from inevitable that I would be identified with where I appear in the story. The fantasy allows or creates a multiplicity of positions within the story between which one can float, shifting from one to the other. At times a form of having it all. But what is held commonplace is the idea that there will be an identification with what the psychoanalysts call the "ego ideal". The place in the narrative where I would appear in the most likeable way. And where would this be? Inside Ditchburn's voluptuous—sorry, *voluminous* shorts? Or in the place of none other than myself, a castrated place, the place of being "cut" down to size. A place of being put in my place by the "ravenous" eyes of the law, thereby accepting the limits of imaginary omniscience, of becoming just like everybody else? Or, as in the pornographic film am I in the place of the exhibition-istic subject, the one who is being fucked. Or do I neither identify with that position nor with the place of the "cutting edge", the sharp-featured adult, but rather with the pretty explicit position of the gaze of my sniggering team mates, all observing this scenario of enjoyment, of someone being fucked.

The psychoanalytic idea is that the desire that is realised or staged in fantasy is not straightforwardly my own. Rather it is the other's desire. Fantasy is the answer to the question "What is wanted of me?", rather than simply addressing the question "What do *I* want?" Or put another way, what am I for the other? As children we are all embedded in a complex network of relations in which we will serve as both a catalyst and the battle-field for the competing desires of those around us. Our mother, our father, our brother and sister will all fight these battles around us. For example mothers will inevitably send messages to their husband, the father, through the care for the son, and so on and so forth. It is possible that we might dimly glimpse something of this, but in most cases we will hardly be aware of it. But one thing is for sure and that is that we will never entirely grasp what kind of "object" we are for our founding others, our parents; what objectives that they might have for us, partly because they don't know themselves. Not entirely.

Hopefully this story of my unfolding entanglement in football doesn't simply collapse into an "I wasn't given sufficient love by my father" whine, which is certainly not what I feel at all. Rather it is a narrative of failed oedipal identification. For in part it concerns this question of "objects". Remember that little object, the football annual, which might appropriately enough be seen as, or reduced to "a sign of love". After all I say as much. Similarly, as a jealous subject, who can say that my enjoyment of this particular gift was not intensified because it came my way and not into the hands of a potentially covetous brother? Is it not possible to see the Wembley story as follows: I want attention from my/the "old man", didn't get any, so exhibitionistically provoke some response, my words, however stupid—infantile even—are taken sufficiently seriously, and all ends in laughter, as if I am to have the last laugh. At last my desire for recognition is satiated. That is or was my unconscious object-ive.

Possibly there is some truth in these ideas but simultaneously the story moves beyond that. Whilst ostensibly I am making a fool of myself, at the same time, it is possible to notice others gaining considerable gratification from the spectacle. A sacrifice of my omniscience celebrated by the cackling classmates allows that there is something in the fantasy that allows the formation of an identity that would satisfy those others. In other words I successfully take up my place as the object of the other's desire.

But things are never as simple as this. Psychoanalysis seeks to disrupt the more common-sense idea of fantasy as a form of hallucinatory wish fulfilment of those desires that might be ruled out or prohibited by the Law. In my claim that the Wembley story is a fantasmatic narrative, which is not to say that I imagined it all or that it never really took place, this crucially involves the installation of the Law. That bony finger ever so politely jabbing me in the shoulder. Through this act, this cut(ting remark), psychoanalysis wants to call this "symbolic castration", I pass through a loss. A loss of my loquacious omniscience—"Lucky rabbit's foot" my arse—and enter into the "symbolic order". Which is another way of saying that I become one of the crowd. The Law, embodied in the form of the adult voice, is the Ideal that is perversely longed for. The desire is to be fully acknowledged by this Law and thereby integrated into its functioning. So it might be claimed that what I felt that I had "lost", had gone astray in some way, was not my father's love, but more crucially this issue of the Law. The Law in this instance is so crucially linked to clarity, a sense of what was going on, the truth. For let us not forget that in my family it was the situation regarding my parents' relationship that was so repeatedly blurred. Nobody was supposed to know what was going on. Although to some extent that has to be true for all families: do we ever entirely know what is going on between our parents, or any other intimate parties for that matter? But in my family it was a conscious, deliberate project. Law becomes the "lost object of desire", which of course implicates both of my parents, not simply my father, which is not in any way to become reproachful. Consciously.

Winnicott was at pains to emphasise that the child who continues to steal from his or her mother's purse is actually engaging in something on the side of health. He emphasised the refusal to give up, the refusal of terminal despair, all buttressed by a continuing search for what had gone missing. In the same way do I engage in the unconscious seeking out of the tap on the shoulder—the arm of the Law—as I continue to dwell in the hope, all the time supplementing the absence via the enactment of the perverse pleasures of the "gob-shite"?

I first took myself off to football a few months after the school trip to Wembley. It was a Saturday afternoon in March soon after my thirteenth birthday. I was mucking about with some friends in the woods that lie between Amersham and Chesham in Buckinghamshire, when suddenly I heard that unmistakeable sound: the intoxicating roar of the crowd. Without further ado our little party scrambled onto our bikes and were off down the hill to "The Meadow" and the delights of Chesham United Football Club. And that was it, from that moment on I "roared" off to football on each and every available Saturday for the rest of my life. Within a year I had taken myself off to Watford, the nearest Football League club, and within another year was eagerly clambering onto football specials out of Euston and St Pancras to watch Spurs in the Midlands. Never missing. If not playing then watching. Although there are occasions when something else takes precedence—curiously psychoanalytic conferences feature quite highly in the "exceptions". And a retrospective sense of a critical element of its enduring fascination, this hold that football has over me, is that it provided not merely a venue for a working out of various confusions with regard to my sexuality but also a community with a built-in structuring principle of the Law. In other words I had found that "lost object of my desire".

Lurking in the back pages of that little annual were something that will always play an enormous part in any football follower's life: the season's fixtures. Sadly, despite our prayers, certain fixities have been seriously eroded. The football magazine *When Saturday Comes* pays homage to a previous era. A world where the year always began in August (well actually before, because those precious fixtures would appear in *Charles Buchan's Football Monthly* in the July issue . . . in those days the first emergence of those crucial details), where Saturdays at 3pm, ten-minute half-times, "twenty to five", or "Sports Report" at five o'clock all felt utterly sacrosanct. As if you knew where you were: football in the winter, cricket in the summer. I notice that I say that I was "mucking about" just prior to this headlong rush into the arms of football. At some level what I was running from was an emotional "muckiness"; something that felt rather messy and somewhat chaotic with regard to what was going on at home. Football in contrast seemed a sanctuary of comparative certainty: "The Meadow", all sun and buttercups, and the fixity of the fixtures.

But inevitably there are problems with all of this, this fantasy with regard to fantasy. Fantasy constitutes the primordial form of storytelling, and we use these stories in order to veil a whole host of original and impossible deadlocks. Psychoanalysis can sometimes appear to propose that we would all be better off if we were able to organise our confused and confusing life experiences into some form of coherent narrative. Which is precisely what I have gone some way towards in response to the question "why football?" Or what is it about football that does it for me? The problem is not merely that some narratives—and mine may be no different—are false, all based on the occlusion of certain unbearable traumas inmixed with the patching over of certain gaps in order to sustain an intelligible flow. Rather the problem lies with *narrative as such* for inevitably it engages in a spurious attempt to resolve certain fundamental antagonisms via a rearrangement of fragments into a temporal succession. A young man, something of a refugee from the Scritti Politi Camden Town punk rock scene, announced that what he wanted to do was to come to run through with me, from his earliest memories to the present, *all* that he could recall; in sequence. And for two years that is exactly the line that he followed, and far be it for me to in any way suggest that all this was an exercise in futility, but nevertheless I think that when he brought matters up to date we both knew that there was still something left to be desired. And I think that this has to be true when it comes to my accounting for my love of, and addiction to football. Another day, another story. But as is probably the case with all love ties, something evades capture. The truth is that I don't really know the answer to these questions, the whys and wherefores. All that I do know is my love of it.

And that is just fine by me.

www.ingramcontent.com/pod-product-compliance
Ingram Content Group UK Ltd.
Pitfield, Milton Keynes, MK11 3LW, UK
UKHW020409010325
455677UK00029B/824

9 781780 491820